The Challenges of
Minoritized Contingent
Faculty in Higher Education

T0285040

NAVIGATING CAREERS IN HIGHER EDUCATION

The success of diverse faculty entering institutions of higher education is shaped by varying factors at both the individual and institutional levels. Gender, race, class, ethnicity, and immigrant generation influence experiences and aspirations of faculty members and administrators. The Navigating Careers in Higher Education series utilizes an intersectional lens to examine and understand how faculty members and administrators navigate careers and their aspirations to succeed. The series will include books that adopt an interdisciplinary, scholarly approach as well as personal testimonies of individuals sharing their own lived experiences, including challenges faced and lessons learned. With a US or global focus, topics include addressing sexism, homophobia, racism, and ethnocentrism; the role of higher education institutions; the effects of growing non-tenure-track faculty; the challenge of research agenda that may be perceived as controversial; maintaining a life-work balance; and entering leadership positions. Additional topics related to careers in higher education are also welcome.

SERIES EDITOR

Mangala Subramaniam, Senior Vice Provost for Faculty Affairs
Virginia Commonwealth University

SERIES COEDITOR

M. Cristina Alcalde, Vice President for Institutional Diversity and Inclusion
Miami University

OTHER TITLES IN THIS SERIES

The Challenges of Minoritized Contingent Faculty in Higher Education

Edna Chun and Alvin Evans

Purdue University Press • West Lafayette, Indiana

Cataloging-in-Publication Data is available from the Library of Congress.
978-1-61249-836-2 (hardback)
978-1-61249-837-9 (paperback)
978-1-61249-838-6 (epub)
978-1-61249-839-3 (epdf)

Cover: melitas/iStock via Getty Images

To Alexander David Chun—"Alex"

The least glamorous, often overlooked components of any system are often the most vital to its proper function.

ALEX CHUN, 2009

CONTENTS

ILLUSTRATIONS

PREFACE

THE GENESIS OF THIS STUDY AROSE FROM THE COAUTHORS' COMBINED FIVE decades of experience as minoritized administrators in higher education leadership within largely white academic institutions. The first author has held leadership positions in human resources and equity at several different types of institutions including large doctoral research universities, master's-level universities, and a major community college system. She has also taught graduate-level courses in human capital management. The second author has held strategic diversity and human resource leadership positions in higher education as well as in a major urban public school district. Both authors have extensive experience in human resource administration, including organizational development, talent management, labor and employee relations, and total rewards. The coauthors have pursued scholarship in the area of diversity and inclusion through intensive study of the higher education workplace for faculty, department chairs, administrators, and staff. It is our hope that this book will share the voices of minoritized contingent faculty and illuminate the tenuous working conditions they face on a daily basis. We also seek to propose solutions that will assist colleges and universities in strengthening the educational process by addressing the structural employment conditions of non-tenure-track faculty including compensation, career ladders, and job security as well as in building more inclusive talent practices.

ACKNOWLEDGMENTS

THIS BOOK IS DEDICATED TO ALEXANDER DAVID CHUN, "ALEX," WHOSE PAS-
sionate and courageous spirit inspires us to continue working to build
more inclusive and equitable organizations. Alex saw beyond the barriers of difference and hierarchy, valuing the voices of each person he encountered, and was known for compassion and care for patients as driving principles in his medical practice. The enthusiasm, creativity, and joy
he brought to medicine, music, and his commitment to the environment
are touchstones for us in our own journeys. Perhaps his own words at
age sixteen in a poem titled "Inner Beauty" sum it up best: "The body is
simply a vehicle from which the mind can soar; Just a home for a heart
and not much more. For however delicate the features of a face may be;
Such outer beauty means nothing if the soul's not free."

We would like to express our sincere gratitude to Professor Mangala
Subramaniam, senior vice provost for faculty affairs at Virginia Commonwealth University, for her great encouragement and help. We also
thank director Justin Race, acquisitions editor Andrea Gapsch, and senior production editor Kelley Kimm at Purdue University Press for their
thoughtful guidance throughout the publication process. We greatly ap-
preciate the suggestions of the anonymous faculty peer reviewers that
have strengthened the manuscript.

We thank all the courageous faculty and administrators who shared
their perspectives on teaching with us as well as their commitment to
the educational process. We are especially indebted to Professor Joe R.
Feagin, Ella C. McFadden Distinguished Professor of Sociology at Texas
A&M University, for his invaluable insights and suggestions throughout the writing of the book. We sincerely thank Bryan Cook, director
of higher education policy at the Urban Institute, for his generous help

on the data analysis; Professor Charles Behling of the University of Michigan (retired) for his important insights; Angela Calise of Ethos Talent for her skilled assistance in data interpretation; and Maricar Cayubit for her expert help on the data displays

Alvin Evans would like to thank his children, Shomari Evans, Jabari Evans, Kalil Evans, and Rashida VanLeer, for their loving support. Edna Chun thanks Jay K. Chun, David S. C. Chu, George S. T. Chu, and Alex Chun's dear friends for their continuous and loving encouragement. Since the completion of this book, Edna Chun has lost her beloved husband, Jay, who so patiently stood by her side for many years, supported her in every endeavor, and above all, unselfishly wanted only the best for his family.

INTRODUCTION

The Impact of COVID-19 and the Defunding of Higher Education on Contingent Faculty

T he tragic story of Thea Hunter, a Black female academic who completed her doctorate in history at Columbia University, illustrates the struggles of adjunct faculty to survive in a tightening economy without sufficient financial resources or health insurance. According to her doctoral adviser, celebrated historian Eric Foner, Hunter's dissertation that focused on the case of James Somerset, a Black man who escaped slavery and won his freedom at trial in England, was a pioneering analysis in the study of transatlantic law and slavery.[1]

Following completion of her dissertation, Dr. Hunter assumed a tenure-line teaching position at Western Connecticut College but left due to a long commute from New York City and an apparently unsatisfying work experience. She faced growing financial difficulties as she alternated between temporary and adjunct appointments, including some not in her own field at several universities. As she wrote in an email, "I have been saying I am done, emotionally drained and without reserves. There has just been too much going on in my life that has been drawing upon whatever emotional reserves I have. That plus the constant financial crisis that has been my life for years takes its toll."[2] Without regular health checkups, this once-promising scholar's asthma and heart condition worsened, and she passed away on December 17, 2018, after being transported to the hospital by ambulance. Her colleagues at Columbia University are memorializing her work by including her papers in an edited collection.[3] Hunter's story reflects the loss to society and waste of scholarly talent due to the highly constricted academic job market.

Thea Hunter's employment circumstances exemplify the precarious and unstable working conditions of non-tenure-track (NTT) teaching faculty. The COVID-19 pandemic that swept the United States in 2020–2021 exposed deep cracks in the academic mission of colleges and universities. As institutions faced drastic budgetary cutbacks due to enrollment declines, loss of tuition revenue, and decreased funding, contingent faculty positions, both full-time and part-time, were among the first to be eliminated. Part-time faculty were the group most affected by the pandemic, with a drop of 5 percent at all institutions and a 6 percent decrease at master's, baccalaureate, and associate degree institutions.[4]

Overall, the workforce experienced a 13 percent loss in what has been described in a *Washington Post* analysis as an "unequal recession" due to its severe impact on the lowest-paid workers.[5] While employees of color make up only one-quarter of the entire higher education workforce, more than half of those laid off were nonwhite.[6] This trend is consistent with a recent research study indicating that women and people of color are more likely to be laid off during times of economic uncertainty. In fact, during the Great Recession of 2007–2009, hiring of Black, Hispanic, and Asian American faculty declined disproportionately in colleges and universities, with public institutions implementing the largest cuts.[7] Crystal Chang, a lecturer at the University of California, Berkeley, summed up the dire circumstances of NTT faculty: "Contingent faculty were already living on the margins before the COVID-19 pandemic. Now we find ourselves at the precipice."[8] The higher education workforce began a slow recovery, building back a third of the 660,000 jobs it had lost by mid-2021.[9]

Public institutions were especially hard hit in the pandemic, with an estimated $74 billion decrease in state funding coupled with additional expenditures of $24 billion for related safety measures.[10] This decimation of budgetary resources is particularly problematic, since public institutions enroll 14.6 million of the nation's 19.7 million students. Funding cuts disproportionately impact students of color and low-income students who enroll in greater numbers in these institutions. Early estimates indicate that enrollment of historically underrepresented students declined at a faster rate during the pandemic than enrollment of historically privileged students.[11]

Notably, states affected by the tourism industry and fossil fuels faced dramatic drops in revenue, resulting in further fiscal retrenchment. For example, the University of Alaska endured three years of budget slashing and program reduction. In early 2020, the university's Board of Regents voted to eliminate, reduce, or merge forty-five academic programs that included undergraduate majors in sociology, chemistry, and earth sciences. In Nevada, a 20 percent cut to higher education in 2020 was followed by an additional 12 percent cut over the biennium.[12] And at the University of Hawaii, the legislature cut the system budget by 10 percent, with a greater share or 14 percent assumed by the flagship Manoa campus. These substantial cuts amounted to $47 million in the first year and $42 million in the second year.[13] All told, the pandemic created budgetary crises at many institutions, both public and private, leading in many cases to cuts in part- and full-time contingent positions.

THE STEADY EROSION OF TENURED FACULTY POSITIONS

The layoffs of contingent faculty during the pandemic struck at the heart of the educational equation, since these faculty now comprise the majority of the instructional workforce. The continuous shrinking of the tenured faculty ranks over the past five decades has resulted in a significant imbalance of teaching resources. Now, nearly three-quarters of faculty are serving in part- and full-time contingent roles. Furthermore, even among this new faculty majority, almost half of the instructional workforce is part-time, with another 20 percent holding full-time contingent positions.[14]

The dramatic increase in contingent faculty employment over the past five decades is not accidental. While it has arisen in some part due to fiscal constraints, the growth in both part- and full-time contingent positions also reflects the perceived benefits of administrative convenience and workforce control. The contingent faculty model now replicates the trend in the US workplace at large toward a gig economy that favors short-term, project-based assignments without employment protections. In their perceptive book *The Gig Academy* (2019), Adrianna Kezar, Tom DePaola, and Daniel Scott solidify the parallels between the gig economy and the gig academy. As they explain, the gig economy is a collection of workforce management approaches and practices that have emanated from neoliberalism. In higher education, these practices center around forms of "at will" and "just-in-time" employment as a major strategy for control and regulation of the workforce.[15] In essence, these practices of administrative control hark back to twentieth-century industrial labor methods of control that limit employees' rights and are justified in terms of cost efficiency and responsiveness to market demands.[16]

The shift to a predominantly contingent faculty workforce has occurred as job opportunities for new PhDs have eroded dramatically. Colleges and universities have capitalized on the oversupply of academically prepared candidates in today's saturated academic job market. In the view of Kezar and colleagues, "the structural lack of stability imposed by the so-called gig economy is a key part of a broader regime for regulating a surplus labor supply, which it has *intentionally fabricated*."[17] What does this mean? Even given the lack of tenured faculty positions, academic institutions have continued unrelentingly to churn out doctoral degrees. In fact, the number of PhDs awarded in the United States doubled from 91,218 in 1976–1977 to 184,000 in 2017–2018.[18] Whether intentional or simply the desire of colleges and universities to sustain enrollment in doctoral programs, the oversupply of PhD recipients means that the practices of short-term faculty and staff employment will continue to thrive.

Note also that the constriction of employment rights for contingent faculty through "at will" appointments substantially limits the exercise of the central component of tenured faculty work, that is, academic freedom. Contingent faculty have few if any safeguards for speaking out and also may have limited input into academic curricular matters. Henry Reichman, chair of the American Association of University Professors' Committee A on Academic Freedom and Tenure, points out that threats to academic freedom have accelerated and are more dangerous than at any time period since the 1950s.[19] Interference in university governance by conservative legislators and corporatized boards of trustees, especially in the public sector, can undermine faculty control of teaching. Faculty members have experienced harassment through online and personal interactions due to controversial comments made in or outside the classroom. The examples of abrupt termination and nonrenewal of adjunct faculty for controversial comments or perceived violations of minor rules are numerous.[20]

What is the appeal of the contingent faculty model to colleges and universities? Contingent faculty appointments allow substantially greater flexibility, represent a limited-term employment commitment, and require investment of far fewer financial resources. Part-time/adjunct faculty can be hired at the last minute by department chairs as course enrollments fluctuate from term to term. To add to the convenience factor, the adjunct recruitment and hiring process usually has few procedural requirements, and department chairs can draw from available pools of individuals in their existing networks without the process requirements and search committees required for tenure-track appointments. Because appointments are essentially discretionary, there is considerable leeway in decision-making, with few checks and balances and the tendency for department chairs and faculty to hire from existing personal networks. These processes often do not involve affirmative action and other standards that help ensure fair employment.[21] And chairs and tenured faculty who prefer to teach upper-division and graduate courses are often responsive to the appeal to deploy contingent faculty to teach large undergraduate sections.

The de-professionalization of contingent faculty roles derives from what scholars describe as a series of "material indignities" that are magnified by economic insecurity.[22] In the words of Mark Purcell, a University of Washington professor who was formerly a contingent faculty member, through "pervasive exclusion, oppression, and devaluation," these faculty are confined to "limbo," a state of being in between, of representing "a spectral, supernatural presence."[23] As he explains, "They are not fully there. They are in limbo in every sense of the word. . . . [T]hey are not really members of the faculty. They are in between. And they are waiting. For something to break. . . . Meanwhile they move in the shadows."[24] Consistent with this perspective, researchers Kim Tolley and Kristen Edwards aptly describe adjuncts and, by extension, contingent faculty as members of a growing "academic precariat."[25] Consider how Sahil, an Asian American male queer adjunct faculty member in a midwestern public research university, describes "the caste system" of two-tiered faculty employment in which even the language used to designate lecturers as compared to professors reifies this distinction: "An interesting thing to really reflect on is how the institution creates that caste system in many ways and then tries to reinforce it in the language they use."

But the so-called case system extends beyond mere nomenclature. Research indicates that the impact of such secondary status in terms of job security, compensation, and health benefits is highly consequential and affects not only career but also life trajectories. In *Dying for a Paycheck* (2018), Stanford University professor Jeffrey Pfeffer identifies and documents ten workplace factors arising from employer decisions that affect health and mortality. Eight of these factors clearly apply to the working conditions of part-time and even some full-time contingent faculty: (1) unemployment as a result of being laid off (or the threat of being laid off), (2) lack of health insurance, (3) working long hours in a week, (4) job insecurity, (5) low control over the job with relatively little discretion, (6) high job demands, (7) low levels of social support, and (8) settings in which employment-related decisions do not seem fair. Based on a meta-analysis of more than two hundred articles by Pfeffer and his colleagues, research reveals that the factors have profound effects on mental and physical well-being and, in turn, affect morbidity, mortality, and health care costs. Strikingly, the meta-analysis found that the absence of health insurance is the leading employment condition that contributes to the greatest number of annual excess deaths, followed by unemployment and then job insecurity.[26] In other words, job insecurity, unemployment or even sporadic employment, and the lack of health insurance affect mortality and life expectancy.

Take the experience of Gila Berryman, a Black English adjunct at the New York City College of Technology. She stopped at the supermarket and had just pulled out her EBT (food stamp) card to pay for groceries when she ran into one of her students who greeted her with "Hi, Professor Berryman." Berryman was averaging $10,000 per year from her part-time course load and had made only $23,000 one year when she took on summer classes and twelve hours of tutoring per week in addition to her full academic year course load, which involved grading six hundred papers. She knew that her students had no understanding of her reality, and a few students even guessed that her annual salary was close to $65,000. In her words,

> I wasn't ashamed of using food stamps to afford groceries. But that day I felt like a fraud. What kind of role model was I? I was a Black woman teaching working-class Black and brown students the importance of learning to write clearly so they could get a good job, yet I couldn't support myself on my own salary.

After a decade of teaching as an adjunct, Berryman experienced a severe case of burnout and left teaching to pursue freelance writing and editing jobs.[27]

The average pay for part-time contingent faculty, or adjuncts, in doctoral institutions is only $1,288 per credit hour and $917 at associate degree institutions.[28] This compensation typically does not account for work outside of class, including classroom preparation, grading papers, and office hours. Adjuncts do not receive the benefit of institutional commitment and support, whether in terms of ongoing employment, health care, training and development, or even obtaining a living wage. Most adjuncts who are paid per course do not have any health insurance or retirement benefits from a plan to which their employer contributed. In 2019–2020, only 30.4 percent of institutions contributed to retirement plans, and only 29.9 percent of institutions contributed to medical insurance premiums.[29] Adjunct appointments are at the mercy of departmental politics and can suffer from budgetary whiplash. Gary Rhoades, professor at the University of Arizona, remarked on the difficulties heightened by the pandemic, stating that adjuncts are "kind of like the Uber drivers. COVID just heightens and surfaces the already existing inequities."[30]

The working conditions for full-time contingent faculty are noticeably better, with longer contracts after initial periods that can range from as little as a semester to three or more years. These full-time roles at least offer some measure of stability, often involving appointments of one or more years and generally including health insurance and other benefits. An increasing number of institutions have developed contingent career ladders with title changes, salary increases, and even continuing status after an extended period. Nonetheless, our interviews reveal that modest pay levels on nine-month contracts at doctoral research institutions that hover around $50,000 for teaching three courses per term can present significant financial challenges. Only small salary adjustments may be offered after an initial time period, and these adjustments remain unchanged for the duration of a multiyear appointment.

For example, Valerie, a Black female full-time contingent faculty member at an eastern liberal arts college, notes the difficult trade-off between staying in a full-time contingent role with limited salary potential and trying to piece together an income as an adjunct at multiple institutions. She concludes that the latter choice would leave her little energy and time to devote to students:[31]

> Sometimes you think this position is going to pay me that, and it doesn't pay you that. And then if you renew the position, you have like a 2 percent increase in your pay that you have to hold on to for the next two or three years or however long your appointment is. So, you have to make a decision: Do I want to walk away or do I want to have five jobs that saturate me in five different places? So then I have 1 percent of myself left to give to twenty-five students in front of me.

The typical workload for a full-time contingent faculty member is three courses per semester, although this configuration can vary significantly and may also involve additional components of service or administrative work. At one public research university, a full-time lecturer is considered to be 88 percent full-time equivalency for the academic year yet teaches a full load of three courses per semester with an additional service block. Ironically, at this university, although considered full time, these faculty are not paid as 100 percent full-time equivalency. In addition, according to a contingent faculty union leader at the university, the service block has grown in a kind of scope creep and includes committee meetings, faculty meetings, and work with students and the community. This teaching load is in stark contrast with tenured faculty at the university, who teach two courses per semester with responsibilities for service and research.

At some institutions, even so-called full-time contingent appointments can involve semester-by-semester variations in full-time equivalency. For example, at another elite western public research university, a full-time appointment can dip in full-time equivalency over the course of a single school year. In such cases, health benefits can terminate especially during the summer months and wreak havoc in terms of needed health care coverage. The faculty member then may need to go through the onerous process of reapplying for coverage in the fall. Consistent with Jeffrey Pfeffer's analysis, the roller coaster in health care coverage can be not only time-consuming and frustrating but also damaging to the health of individuals and their families.

With these prevailing workforce realities in mind, it is clear that the two-tiered faculty structure constitutes a significant inequality regime within higher education. Scholars Donald Tomaskovic-Dewey and Dustin Avent-Holt indicate that inequality regimes vary at the workplace level, are not uniform, and depend on unequal power that has been routinized and reproduced through the medium of unequal employment conditions.[32] Moreover, as social theorist Joe Feagin points out, institutions and processes that reproduce social inequality are grounded in relationships that are fundamentally inegalitarian, asymmetrical, and oppositional. Powerlessness is a key feature replicated in contingent faculty status and is emblematic of well-developed and long-standing systems of oppression.[33]

Asymmetrical power arising from status differentials is exacerbated when individuals in secondary academic positions are from different cultural and social identities than those in authority.[34] As a result, contingent faculty can experience double marginalization due to their secondary employment status in the academic hierarchy coupled with the exclusion resulting from minoritized social identities. When coupled with minoritized status, contingent faculty often must struggle for acceptance, recognition, and career stability in the day-to-day academic environment and can face devaluation of their contributions.

Perceptions of incompetence can limit their contributions, opportunity, and mobility with significant material, social, and psychological outcomes.[35] Yet remarkably, only recently have accounts of the experiences of Black, Indigenous, and People of Color (BIPOC) in contingent faculty roles even begun to come to light. For example, Takumi Sato, an Asian American cisgender male NTT faculty member at a predominantly white institution, documents the racial battle fatigue he experienced resulting from being ignored, pacified, and deflected within academe as a person of color. He acknowledges that he was inadequately prepared for the tactics used against him and underestimated the extent to which systematic oppression permeated academic spaces.[36]

INTERLOCKING DIMENSIONS OF EXCLUSION

Based on extensive research and our own interview findings, in this book we posit that the intersectionality of minoritized social identities including race, gender, sexual orientation, gender identity, disability, age, class, and religion can compound and intensify experiences of marginalization and exclusion for contingent faculty. In the higher education environment, scholars have recognized the unique experiences that derive from the intersectionality of social identities and the ways in which membership in different identity groups can affect how individuals are perceived and treated on college campuses.[37]

Yet, as Fred Bonner, professor and chair of educational leadership at Prairie View A&M University, explains, intersectionality has "fallen woefully short in providing an authentic rendering of the experiences of Black men and boys." Bonner suggests the term "mascu'sectionality" as a possible alternative theoretical framework for Black males. This approach does not negate feminist perspectives but instead seeks a viable approach to the experiences of Black men. He cites the challenges of using intersectionality as a critical lens to evaluate the experiences of Black men who are presumed to share the advantages of patriarchy and, when they do not, are seen as somehow deviant.[38] In this regard, consider how Justin, a Black male clinical sociology faculty member in an elite western private university, describes the double marginalization he faces as a contingent faculty member and a scholar on social justice and race:

> It's twofold. . . . [M]y place in the hierarchy in terms of tenure. . . .
> [T]hat's part of the pie. The other half would have to be . . . because
> I am who I am and what I am talking about: this idea of calling out
> social justice and race, talking about intersectionality, talking about
> the white racial frame. That's beyond them. . . . So I think you are iso-
> lated because of skin tone but also by the manner in which I speak
> for equality and justice and point out the wrongs within systems in
> organizations.

Reinforcing Bonner's observation, Justin indicates that because he is a Black male speaking about racism, others may feel discomfort, as he is forcing them "to look in that mirror" in terms of their relationship to white supremacy and systemic oppression. Justin's keen description of his vulnerable positionality in the academic hierarchy sheds light on the double jeopardy faced by minoritized contingent faculty. While be-ing male is not usually described as a minoritized identity, being a Black male has vastly different connotations and has led to extensive stereo-typing in the United States. As Justin explains,

> You know, I'm dealing with a two-edged sword. One due to the stereo-
> types and thoughts about a Black male . . . and the lack of real power
> as a contingency sort of instructor. I think I'm challenged more than
> I would be if I was a white male or if I was a white female or if I was
> a Black female as well.

The pioneering work of sociologist Patricia Hill Collins provides a ho-listic framework for understanding the impact of intersectionality and systems of power on minoritized contingent faculty in the higher education workplace. Her analysis highlights the "cognitive architecture" of intersectionality in terms of the overlapping core constructs of relationality, power, social inequality, social context, complexity, and social justice. The guiding premises of this framework clarify how these interlocking systems of power reinforce each other, yield complex social inequalities, and shape the differential experiences of both individuals and groups.[39]

The concept of relationality refers to the interdependence of race, gender, class, and other systems of power and the ways that these systems mutually construct each other. According to Collins, examination of the ways in which multiple structures of domination intersect allows "a clearer view of oppression," since, for example, minority women cannot use whiteness to neutralize the stigma of being Black or maleness to negate female subordination.[40] Columbia University professor Kimberlé Crenshaw further cautions against thinking about subordination as occurring along a single axis or category causing distortion in which, for example, Black women "are theoretically erased."[41]

In this regard, a study of fifty-nine Black female executives in the corporate sector offers significant insight into the phenomenon of intersectional invisibility in which individuals from two or more nondominant groups are both physically hypervisible and cognitively invisible. These executives experienced the tendency to be consistently overlooked, forgotten, or disregarded even as they held positions in the upper four levels of their organizations. Michaela, a managing director of financial services, described the challenge of having "a boss who really gives you no airtime, cancels every meeting, doesn't give you a sense of belonging." In navigating intersectional invisibility, the female executives have had to focus on the development of professional identities that aligned with others' expectations for their leadership in order to disconfirm negative stereotypes. The lack of acceptance in these roles has led them to scrutinize and carefully construct their professional image by focusing on style, appearance, and related factors.[42]

Another eye-opening study of 423 corporations, "Women in the Workplace 2021," found that women of color and women with other traditionally marginalized identities face a wider and more frequent range of microaggressions at work that cast them as outsiders. In addition, they receive less support and are twice as likely to feel burned out and three times as likely to report struggling to concentrate at work due to stress. Tellingly, the study reveals that women who are "the only" or "double onlys" in a workplace face greater discrimination, bias, and pressure to perform.[43]

Furthermore, the exclusion experienced by minoritized contingent faculty may in some cases be an extension of socially imposed barriers that individuals have experienced previously in the educational process. Several of our interviewees described the challenges they faced as first-generation college students coming from immigrant or low-income backgrounds. While in graduate school, they did not have any assistance from influential faculty sponsors in navigating the complex requirements of doctoral education or in subsequently obtaining a coveted tenure-track position. For example, Sahil, the Asian American queer contingent faculty member cited earlier, describes how his undergraduate experiences and the lack of sponsorship in unfamiliar academic environments substantially affected his later career trajectory:

> I really struggled as an undergraduate student. And I think because of that, I, you know, didn't pursue things like an independent study; I didn't write an honors thesis. I didn't have the best relationships with my faculty because they didn't reflect my identities or they were not as inclusive as I would have hoped that they were. And so, I think those things prevented me from going straight into a PhD program. I think my identity impacted it in terms of long-term trajectory. So, I think that, you know, if I had more privileged identities I probably would have a PhD by now and hopefully, you know, have a tenure-track position.

Tressie McMillan Cottom, professor at the University of North Carolina–Chapel Hill, further emphasizes that the perils of adjunctification are intensified for Black contingent faculty. These faculty may have already encountered significant structural barriers in the educational process leading to their subsequent difficulty in attaining tenured positions. In fact, Cottom sees adjunctification as a pathway to poverty: "Adjunct labor in higher education has revealed the structural flaw in our post-recession reality: The prescription for poverty—educational attainment—has become a condition *for* poverty."[44] In other words, the very myth of progress through educational attainment for underrepresented groups has led to an uncertain career pathway that can result in poverty and lack of stable employment.

THE EXPENDABLE NATURE OF CONTINGENT FACULTY APPOINTMENTS

Consider the ways that the pandemic has laid bare the underlying scaffolding of faculty inequality in the two-tiered employment model. The stories of contingent faculty losing their positions during the pandemic were so widespread that the *Chronicle of Higher Education* ran a special article titled "Forced Out" in April 2021. These reports of contingent faculty layoffs are just the most prominent instances that surfaced in press accounts. The devastating experiences of contingent faculty underscore their precarious working conditions, financial challenges, psychological demoralization, and the loss of identity that can result from nonrenewal. In some cases, individuals were already well advanced in their careers with few prospects of finding new positions. Ageism can impinge upon the career prospects of more senior faculty in a severely constrained academic job market. Just as significant, however, is the impact of the layoffs on the student educational experience and the loss to the scope and richness of educational programs. As academic programs are downsized or even eliminated, students lose the opportunity to pursue important fields of interest and work closely with valued faculty mentors.

Among the shattering accounts included in the *Chronicle of Higher Education* article is that of Zoe Fox, math lecturer at the University of Illinois at Chicago. Fox (who uses the pronouns they, them, and theirs), described the emotional toll of not being reappointed in the fall of 2020 after two years of working at the institution. When told while teaching a summer course that there were no jobs, Fox described entering the first of the five stages of grief. Still retaining hope for reappointment, Fox penned a letter to department leaders that ultimately received no response.

Upon finally receiving notice of nonreappointment in the summer of 2020, Fox cried at the news but still had to show up to teach classes the next day. As Fox explained, "Losing your job is one of these cultural touchstones where everybody knows it sucks, but you don't actually realize how humiliating and terrifying it is until it happens to you."[45] Later, after living on unemployment insurance and a stipend from the faculty union, Fox found a job as a staff organizer for the university's graduate union. The realization that faculty are expendable and that the university is run like a business became clear to Fox from this experience. In Fox's poignant words, "Cutting costs means cutting me."

The working conditions at the University of Illinois at Chicago for contingent faculty are quite typical. Although both part- and full-time contingent faculty at the university are represented by the United Faculty union, the contract only requires notification of renewal (or nonrenewal) of fall NTT appointments by the preceding June 1. Little recourse exists for appeal or reconsideration. Yet, when fully 5 percent of NTT faculty were not renewed in 2020, the union submitted a letter of protest signed by 250 faculty and allies to the university administration. When no response was forthcoming, the union began to pressure the Board of Trustees by holding a press conference and sending a letter timed to coincide with the board meeting. In the press conference, Jeff Schuhrke, a visiting lecturer and contingent faculty member, emphasized the prevailing administrative view that NTT faculty are disposable and expendable in a system that creates anxiety and uncertainty and therefore hurts the students who rely on these faculty.[46]

Other stories of contingent faculty layoffs reverberated across the educational landscape, with a particularly significant toll taken on small liberal arts colleges. Take the situation of Lenora Warren, an African American and Latina lecturer in the Department of English at Ithaca College who was laid off from her teaching position in African American literature. Warren holds a PhD in English from New York University and had left a tenure-track position at Colgate University to be with her husband, who is executive director of the Cornell Prison Education Program. Warren's academic achievements include a book on abolitionism and insurrection in the eighteenth and nineteenth centuries. When notified of the nonrenewal of her contingent teaching position, she found herself "demoralized" with "a sense of total identity loss." She was perplexed at how the college claimed to believe in diversity but was cutting that part of the curriculum. Discouraged and dispirited, Warren stopped attending the administration's faculty forums once she realized that "the 'we' being referenced were the ones who were staying, whose jobs were safe—not the ones being fired. It isn't even my college anymore."[47]

On of the most egregious cases of contingent faculty nonrenewals during the pandemic was the massive layoff of 2,800 adjunct faculty and 1 part-time staff in the twenty-five-campus system of the City University of New York (CUNY). Announced on July 1, 2020, this sweeping action underscored the vulnerability of part-time instructional faculty despite their long-standing contributions to the institutions they served. As was the situation at a number of other institutions, the timing of the layoffs occurred amid an already bleak employment situation and appeared to contradict the commitment to employees that should have been at the forefront of institutional human resources policy.

The impersonal way the layoffs were communicated reinforced the disposable nature of adjunct faculty appointments. Significant prior service to the institutions by these faculty appeared to have minimal impact. For example, longtime adjuncts such as Bernard A. Bilawsky at Queensborough Community College, who had taught business courses for forty-eight years as a "temporary" employee, were only sent a three-line form email about their reappointment.[48] As Bilawsky recounts,

> Along with hundreds of other adjuncts, at the end of June, I received a three-line form email from the college HR director informing me that I would not be reappointed for the fall semester. My years as an adjunct started in the spring semester of 1972. Yes, that's correct. Forty-eight years ago I became a "temporary" employee. Since that time, I was offered courses each semester by each of the department's four different chairpersons, until now. I received not a personal word in regard to my impending departure from the college. Nothing. *Not from the department chair and not from the director of HR, in spite of both of them knowing me for decades.*

Monika Pacholcyk, adjunct lecturer at LaGuardia Community College and Baruch College, also described her nonreappointment as "extended agony" after more than twenty years at LaGuardia and twelve years at Baruch. At age fifty-three, Pacholcyk lost her health insurance and had to pay the rent for her one-bedroom Queens apartment with unemployment insurance and cover her burgeoning medical expenses with Medicaid.[49]

Even prior to the pandemic, adjunct salaries at CUNY had made it difficult to earn a subsistence-level living in New York City. As Rose Squillacote, adjunct assistant professor of political science at Hunter College, observed, "Currently, if I were to work 'full-time' as an adjunct (and my earnings are in the higher range of what adjuncts make), teaching six classes a year, I would make $30,000 a year pre-tax—about $19 an hour."[50]

Pushback to CUNY's large-scale downsizing of the contingent faculty ranks occurred at a subsequent hearing held by the Higher Education, Civil Service, and Labor Committees of the New York City Council in November 2020. CUNY's senior vice chancellor and chief financial officer, Matthew Sapienza, testified that despite the receipt by CUNY of $251 million from the federal government in the 2020 Coronavirus Aid, Relief, and Economic Security Act, the cuts were justified by a 5.1 percent drop in enrollment, with additional expenses arising from the pandemic and a state budget cut by Governor Andrew Cuomo of $2 billion, or 20 percent of the budget.[51]

Unsatisfied by this explanation, city council Higher Education Committee chair Inez Barron pressed Sapienza and Pamela Silverblatt, senior vice chancellor for labor relations, further: "We know that CUNY relies on adjuncts for the bulk of the instruction," she said. "So why are we now gutting that body that is responsible for delivering that instruction?" And Barbara Bowen, president of the Professional Staff Congress/CUNY that represents the employees, chastised the university for its rush to lay off adjuncts: "They rushed to lay off adjuncts even before cuts were applied, revealing the deep structural problem of contingency."[52]

The financial justification offered by Sapienza for the large-scale layoffs was later seriously undercut when a proposal to hire the McKinsey Corporation for a $3 million no-bid consulting contract to develop a plan for reopening the university was set to come to a vote at the April 2021 board meeting. After a tidal wave of public pressure, the proposal was pulled from the agenda at the last minute.[53] CUNY's mixed message of considering multimillion-dollar consulting contracts while conducting layoffs of low-paid adjuncts appeared to be at odds with its long-standing commitment to provide education to working-class families. In fact, the median household income of CUNY students is less than $40,000 a year, and 38 percent of the students come from households earning less than $20,000 per year.[54]

In another prominent example of mass adjunct layoffs during the pandemic, Rutgers University (also known as the State University of Jersey) asked its adjunct workforce to help transition to remote instruction in the spring of 2020. Yet, after the adjuncts pitched in and retooled for the change, when the pandemic struck Rutgers did not rehire three hundred adjuncts for the next academic year. This move was particularly astonishing, since 30 percent of undergraduate courses at Rutgers are taught by part-time adjuncts. Critics noted that the cost of rehiring the adjuncts for both the fall and spring semesters was less than the salary of the head football coach, who was earning $4 million in the first year of an eight-year contract.[55] Once again, we see a disconnection between claims of financial difficulties when it comes to the meager salaries of part-time faculty and the willingness to spend exorbitant sums of money for other administrative purposes.

Compounding the difficulties, on a number of college campuses a clear blow was delivered to faculty labor unions as universities and colleges invoked fiscal exigency clauses to justify faculty layoffs. Between 2013 and 2019, significant growth in the unionization of contingent faculty in both public and private universities had occurred, with 118 newly certified bargaining units and a total of 36,264 members added between 2013 and 2019.[56] The pandemic revealed the inability of collective bargaining units to protect faculty, both tenured and nontenured, in the face of budget crises, resulting in the wholesale elimination of majors, programs, and departments. Although NTT faculty have union representation at both Rutgers and CUNY, fiscal exigency and emergency clauses in their contractual agreements permitted the implementation of large-scale layoffs. In another example, at the University of Akron the arbitrator, Jack Buettner, ruled in binding arbitration that the "catastrophic circumstances" permitted the elimination of unionized faculty positions, including tenured faculty incumbents.[57] After the dust settled, 67 faculty were laid off, and 21 retired or voluntarily resigned.[58] In spite of these difficult financial circumstances, researchers indicate that

NTT faculty have been important catalysts for change on college campuses particularly at the localized level.[59]

Looking at the bigger picture, many public universities and colleges including Rutgers, CUNY, and the University of Akron have suffered from the continuous shrinking of state support. As we shall discuss further in chapter 1, declining state support for public higher education has caused colleges and universities to make up budgetary shortfalls with increased tuition and fees. Today, tuition and fees represent the major source of revenue for public higher education.[60]

QUESTIONS THE BOOK SEEKS TO ANSWER

Although a substantial body of research has focused on the working conditions of contingent faculty over the past few decades, scant attention has been paid to the differential experiences of minoritized faculty in these roles. The dilemmas posed by a rapidly changing academic landscape and increased hostility to diversity in the United States have intensified the challenges for contingent faculty from minoritized groups. Due to the very limited literature on the experiences of minoritized contingent faculty, this book seeks to explore the disparate workplace realities encountered by these faculty in both part- and full-time NTT roles. Our research focuses on four-year institutions both private and public, although we include associate degree colleges with four-year degrees in the overall data analysis shared in chapter 2.

The book focuses on the following policy and research questions:

1. How have neoliberal trends, political partisanship, and a tightening of administrative control in colleges and universities accelerated the movement to a two-tiered faculty instructional model?
2. What are the discrete challenges faced by minoritized faculty in contingent roles? How has the intersectionality of minoritized characteristics such as race, gender, sexual orientation, gender

identity, first-generation status, disability, and age affected their employment experiences?

3. What specific strategies have assisted minoritized contingent faculty in coping with the stress and precariousness of their employment status?

4. How can institutions adopt proactive workforce strategies and policies to address the employment conditions of contingent faculty?

Our primary audience for the book is presidents, provosts, chief financial officers, academic and administrative leaders, department chairs, tenure-line and contingent faculty, and diversity officers as well as those involved in university strategic planning initiatives and staffs of state/local legislative entities responsible for supporting academic goals.

METHODOLOGY FOR THE STUDY

An extensive literature review was undertaken for the book, including a broad range of resources on contingent faculty and the limited research pertaining to the experiences of minoritized contingent faculty. We approached the existing literature on contingent faculty using extended case methodology to formulate the questions asked and assess the findings from twenty in-depth interviews conducted with contingent faculty and diversity officers/administrators. The extended case method focuses on "theoretical gaps or silences" in the literature that may result from overlooking or failing to address particular aspects of empirical phenomena.[61] Specifically, we found that while the existing literature largely addresses overall working conditions for contingent faculty, only a partial understanding of these conditions can be obtained without examining the impact of minoritized social identities and intersectionality on work experiences. As such, our book seeks to expand and amplify existing theory on the tenuous employment conditions of contingent faculty and illustrate how minoritized social identities including race, gender, sexual orientation, gender identity, disability, age, class, and religion can intensify experiences of marginalization and exclusion. We draw further from the interpretive case method in examining the details derived from our interview findings to illuminate larger macro-realities in the higher education workplace.[62]

Take, for example, the reverse discrimination complaint filed by a white male student against one of our interviewees, Monica, the only Black female lecturer in her department in a largely white midwestern research university. The student escalated the complaint to the provost when he received a grade of B instead of an A. As we detail further in chapter 3, the parents of the student refused to believe that Monica had a doctorate and claimed that she had lied about her qualifications. The mother of the student wrote a note claiming that the family was not racist, stating, "We have black people in our family so we couldn't possibly be racist." Monica's colleagues did not understand the extent to which the situation derived from her minoritized identity. As Monica herself observed, "I think it would have been different if I were a man. . . . Obviously it was about race and so the intersection of race and gender." The data from this interview enhances our understanding of the precarious nature of contingent faculty appointments by revealing how such contingency can be magnified by the intersectionality of minoritized identities.

In this study we refer to NTT faculty as part- or full-time contingent faculty. The term "adjunct" is also used to describe part-time contingent faculty. The terms "clinical professor" and "professor of practice" refer to an NTT appointment in which the faculty member's work involves practical instruction of students such as in medicine, law, and engineering.

All but one of the interviews were conducted virtually via Zoom over an eight-month period between May and December 2021; one interview was via telephone. The interview questions covered the terms of the interviewees' appointments and their experiences in teaching. Open-ended questions were posed relating to appointment renewal, course assignments, student evaluations, and relationship with the department chair, as were questions regarding possible differential treatment based on social identities. The interviews were conducted by the first author, and notes on the salient points of the transcripts were compared by the coauthors. The interviews were approximately one hour in length. Informed consent was obtained for interviewing purposes, and the participants were assured of their confidentiality. All but three of the interviewees chose to remain anonymous. The interviewees were provided transcribed passages selected for use in the study for their review and permission. A profile of the interviewees and a summary of key demographic data are included in the appendix.

Analysis of data from the Integrated Postsecondary Education Data System served as the basis for the summary tables in chapter 2. We focused on full- and part-time contingent faculty data from four-year institutions including associate degree institutions that include baccalaureate degrees, analyzed data by institutional type, and examined the relationship of full-time tenure-line faculty to contingent faculty over a five-decade period.

We begin our study in chapter 1 by examining the systemic factors that have led to the evolution of a two-tiered faculty model. In order to understand this consequential shift, we focus on the progressive impact of the forces of neoliberalism. In this context, we highlight the troubling convergence of diminished funding for public higher education by conservative state legislatures with rising student diversity.

1

How Did We Get Here? Neoliberalism and the Two-Tiered Faculty Equation

Budgets reflect administrative priorities and
political choices, not economic realities.

CRYSTAL CHANG, "HOW THE PANDEMIC HAS PUSHED
CONTINGENT FACULTY TO THE PRECIPICE"

How has the educational situation morphed so dramatically that the very stability of tenured faculty employment is now in danger? In this chapter we explore the ways in which the progressive tide of neoliberalism has permeated institutional structures, employment models, curricular emphases, organizational culture, and decision-making processes. We trace the steady rise of the two-tiered faculty model with its ramifications for college budgets and student learning. Surprisingly, the impact of this massive structural change on the employment conditions of contingent faculty and particularly minoritized faculty and the relation to student learning outcomes has gained relatively little research attention in a number of recent in-depth studies of neoliberalism in higher education.[1]

With the crystallization of neoliberalism and market-based practices in the contingent faculty employment model, a gradual and troubling devaluation of teaching and the educational experience is clearly well under way. In *The Great Mistake* (2016), Christopher Newfield sums up the problematic shift in educational spending and the shift away from instruction in public higher education: "The public university is failing, not because it spends too much money on its core activities of teaching and research, but because it spends too little on them."[2] Henry Giroux similarly notes the perils arising from the neoliberal casualization of academic labor reflected in the increasing numbers of part-time faculty, with a weakened faculty demoralized by the loss of rights and power. While his extensive research on neoliberalism in higher education is less focused on the experiences of contingent faculty, Giroux nonetheless describes the working conditions of adjunct and nontenured faculty as similar to indentured servants who are overworked and underpaid and often lack benefits.[3]

With these insights in mind, we now delve further into the threat posed by the damaging spread of conservative neoliberal practices in higher education and government institutions such as state legislatures. In this context, we examine the large-scale restructuring of the academic workforce through reconfiguration of the faculty role and the increased corporatization of the academic landscape.

THE UNDERPINNINGS OF NEOLIBERALISM

The gradual transformation of the academic landscape has not occurred in a vacuum and reflects the assimilation of neoliberal norms within the culture of higher education over the past half century. In the decades after World War II, the view of higher education as a public good was linked to the attainment of a democratic society for all Americans. But this perspective began to shift with the emergence of neoliberal economic thought in the 1950s and 1960s. In the aftermath of civil rights legislation, a shift to themes of privatization, individual choice, and education as a private good emerged in the context of broader social equality in the United States.[4] The social role of public higher education as enabling the upward mobility for underserved citizens was replaced by an economic view of higher education linked to corporate global competitiveness.[5]

Neoliberalism arose as a counterrevolution in response to what some perceived as governmental social welfare–type reforms undertaken based on the economic theory of John Maynard Keynes. Proponents of Keynesian thought viewed government intervention and investment perspective as necessary to address major economic recessions and stimulate consumer demand.[6] The Keynesian economic perspective was called into question in the aftermath of "stagflation," or high inflation and high unemployment, as rates of profit for US businesses began to drop from 1965 to 1973. Responding to these economic developments, neoliberal economists reignited the emphasis on free market capitalism, which they associated with individual freedom, privatization, and reduction of governmental regulations particularly in relation to corporations. Yet, the net effect of the neoliberal counterrevolution was to increase the power of large corporations in both public and private life. Turning to the past and the perceived benefits of free markets, neoliberal thinkers sought to rejuvenate economic treatises such as Adam Smith's *The Wealth of Nations* (1782). Ironically, however, Smith himself had cautioned against the dangers of large corporations and monopolies that limited market competition. He viewed small businesses as essential to the cultivation of free markets.[7] Further, as David Harvey points out, the role of government was seen as providing an institutional framework that supported oligopoly capitalism, and this framework in turn perpetuated wealth inequality.[8] Neoliberalism inconsistently relied on the executive, legislative, and judicial powers of the state to reconfigure free markets by guaranteeing monetary stability, reducing corporate taxation, and eliminating governmental regulations.[9]

At its heart, neoliberalism was more than simply an economic movement and an espousal of the principles of free market capitalism. It occurred as a sociopolitical response to breakthroughs in racial equality that took place with the *Brown v. Board of Education* school desegregation decisions of 1954 and 1955 and the Civil Rights Act of 1964.[10] Just as public spaces became more accessible to Blacks and other minorities, some whites sought to protect private spaces and retain these spaces as separate and segregated. Sociologist Randolph Hohle aptly identifies the binary of white private/Black public as the underlying paradigm in these systematic efforts.[11]

Neoliberal policymakers advocated for privatization programs in various arenas including public education and also sought to reduce governmental social reforms. At the same time, neoliberals lobbied to reduce governmental deregulation in corporate spheres and pressed for the "upward redistribution" of economic returns, including those from state entities, into the pockets of businesses and elite stakeholders.[12] With the emphasis on the reduced role of the public sector, neoliberals also sought to stem the influence and power of labor unions. In what has been termed "a postwelfare model of capitalism," neoliberal efforts have been directed toward reducing protections for workers and eroding collective bargaining.[13]

Mid-twentieth-century neoliberal thinkers such as the Nobel Prize–winning University of Chicago economist Milton Friedman espoused individual economic liberty, limited government, and consumer choice in the context of a competitive marketplace. Friedman argued against the subsidization of educational institutions, believing that funding institutions "has led to an indiscriminate subsidization of institutions rather than of people."[14] In his view, funding should go to individual students, not state governments, a view that later prevailed in the Educational Amendments of 1972 and the determination by Congress to distribute Pell Grants to individual students rather than institutions.

The critique of higher education by Republican lawmakers and the tightening of budgetary purse strings has been accompanied by calls for greater public accountability in the educational process. This focus has led in turn to the introduction of market-like metrics focused on efficiency particularly as measured in financial terms.[15] State performance-based funding systems have been adopted by thirty state governments, although some were discontinued temporarily. Due to the metrics employed, some institutions have chosen to admit fewer disadvantaged students in order to raise academic requirements and also have focused on high schools with more middle- and upper-class white students.[16] These critiques have also drawn attention to low teaching loads for full-time faculty and the prevalent emphasis on research over teaching.[17]

DECLINING STATE FUNDING AND RISING STUDENT DIVERSITY

With the advent of neoliberalism, we chart the convergence of two important trends in public higher education: the substantial decrease in budgetary appropriations by conservative state legislatures that occurred just as student racial diversity increased. In a recent book, Edna Chun and social theorist Joe Feagin posit that the decline in state funding for higher education by conservative legislatures is linked to the demographic shift in student enrollment as increasingly diverse cohorts of students have enrolled in colleges and universities.[18]

Whereas in 1980 four out of every five students at public institutions including two-year colleges were white, by 2015 slightly more than one of every two students was a student of color.[19] Between 2007 and 2017 alone, the proportion of undergraduate students of color grew from 28 percent to 45 percent.[20] From a rather draconian standpoint, Herb Childress observes that the contingent faculty model is now "a standard operating feature of a system of higher education" explicitly configured to provide different levels of service to different populations. Elite universities and selective liberal arts colleges employ fewer contingent faculty, while at lesser-tier institutions, the majority of faculty are contingent.[21]

Empirical research by Barrett Taylor, Brendan Cantwell, and their colleagues solidifies the clear connection between partisan affiliations related to racial identity under unified Republican governments and a decline in state appropriations.[22] Specifically, under unified Republican control of the state gubernatorial and legislative branches, growth in the enrollment of underrepresented students is substantially correlated with deeper cuts in state appropriations compared to states with a larger representation of white students.[23] The impact of racial resentment can be postulated, given that Republican and Republican-leaning voters are mostly white, with 86 percent white representation in 2016.[24]

Witness the unrelenting decrease in state funding to higher education in eighteen of the forty years between 1980–1981 and 2018–2019.[25] Between 2008 and 2019 alone, state cuts in higher education amounted to $34 billion, with thirty-seven states reducing per-student funding and six states cutting appropriations by more than 30 percent. By 2017, most state colleges and universities had reached an unfortunate milestone when they obtained more of their funding from tuition than from governmental appropriations.[26] If the present trend continues, by 2059 state funding could reach zero.[27] At the same time, average tuition at four-year colleges rose by $2,576, or 35.2 percent, and in ten states by more than 50 percent.[28] These increases have reflected the need to offset budgetary losses. But the increasing tuition costs have disproportionately affected students of color and working-class students, as shown in a study of 597 public institutions. In fact, one study found that a $1,000 increase in tuition was correlated with a drop of 4.5 percent in campus diversity among full-time first-year students.[29]

The financial situation is not improving. In its fiscal year 2020 report, the State Higher Education Officers Association noted that in all likelihood public colleges and universities now face more precarious financial circumstances than at any time in recent history. Tuition revenue in fiscal year 2020 failed to keep pace with the rate of inflation as student enrollment declined in thirty-five states, with the most severe declines in public two-year institutions. The report warns that "continuing to use higher education as a *budgetary release valve* as state economies recover from the pandemic recession may undermine student affordability and harm public institutions' ability to provide quality educational opportunities."[30] According to one financial projection, decreased enrollment, loss of tuition revenue, declining international student enrollment, and suspension of athletic programs could result in revenue losses of $85 billion in fiscal year 2021.

Given these factors, we have also seen how the COVID-19 pandemic heightened employment insecurity for contingent faculty, who are usually the first to be laid off in the face of budgetary shortfalls. This trend is particularly ominous in terms of the looming issues posed by continued reductions in state funding by conservative legislatures. Further, the trend has significant implications for the educational experiences of the growing cohort of diverse students in terms of the loss of faculty role models from minoritized groups.

During the course of the pandemic, the federal government did step in to alleviate the budgetary situation and provide much-needed temporary investments to higher education. Three successive stimulus packages were passed: the Coronavirus Aid, Relief, and Economic Security Act of 2020 and the Coronavirus Response and Relief Supplemental Appropriations Act of 2020, signed by President Donald Trump, and the American Rescue Plan Act of 2021, signed by President Joe Biden. These three pieces of legislation passed by Congress provided significant infusions to the Higher Education Emergency Relief Fund of nearly $14 billion, $20 billion, and $40 billion, respectively.[31] Under all three stimulus packages, half of the funds allotted by the Higher Education Emergency Relief Fund had to be distributed to students through emergency grants.

Interestingly, the stimulus funding did counteract regressive state funding trends by addressing the disparate needs of low-income students and minority-serving institutions. Distribution of funding occurred through the Title IV system based on percentages of Pell Grant recipients at each institution. All three bills included allocations specifically designated for historically Black colleges and universities, tribal colleges, and minority-serving institutions. Without the stimulus funds and due to the precipitous decline in state tax revenues, states would have cut spending to higher education by 2.3 percent. Nonetheless, the ways the states have spent the stimulus funds have varied.[32] Yet, an analysis by the State Higher Education Officers Association cited earlier emphasizes that while these three pieces of legislation did provide significant temporary assistance, this funding does not replace the ongoing need for unrestricted state operating support to public institutions.[33]

With these financial realities at the forefront, we turn now to discuss the forces that have led to the reconfiguration of the traditional faculty portfolio and the progressive decoupling of teaching, research, and service leading to the subordination of undergraduate students in terms of institutional priorities.

RECONFIGURATION OF THE FACULTY ROLE

Over time, the permeation of the neoliberal agenda in higher education and a number of concurrent external influences have led to a narrower conceptualization of faculty work, resulting in the progressive unbundling of teaching, advising, service, and research activities. In large part, the erosion of the traditional faculty model occurred due to funding cuts and the rebalancing of financial portfolios to address revenue shortfalls and replace lost revenue with tuition income. Progressive defunding of public higher education has led to the effort to lower costs in the face of declining student enrollment and increased competition for students.[34] Other factors identified in this major shift include the growth of community colleges beginning in the 1960s and the increasing presence of for-profit institutions.[35]

In the process of unbundling, the role of teaching has been segregated from the traditional components of research, teaching, and service that were articulated in Ernest Boyer's landmark publication *Scholarship Reconsidered* (1990). Boyer recognized the need for differentiation of faculty roles based on institutional type while also supporting the idea of the complete scholar in terms of the triumvirate of research, teaching, and service. As he stated, "What we urgently need today is a more inclusive view of what it means to be a scholar—a recognition that knowledge is acquired through research, through synthesis, through practice, and through teaching."[36] In other words, all dimensions of faculty work contribute to the effectiveness of scholars and inform student learning.

The unbundling of the faculty role in which contingent faculty are almost exclusively involved in teaching has garnered significant institutional cost savings due to the relatively low salaries of contingent faculty in comparison to tenured faculty. This generalized unbundling was not typically guided by research on teaching and learning but instead was accelerated by factors such as the growth of community colleges and for-profit institutions, the need for expanded access to higher education, and the increased professionalization of roles in administrative areas such as student affairs.[37]

Unbundling has also had clear administrative benefits in terms of fiscal and workforce control, as it allows for optimization of faculty resources and undercuts professional entitlements that result from collective faculty decision-making.[38] In addition, unbundling has created at-will working conditions for contingent faculty that closely resemble those of most administrators, and these conditions substantially enhance administrative control.

Most importantly, the contingent faculty model depreciates the value of teaching by failing to recognize its centrality to educational mission. In essence, teaching the undergraduate core curriculum is often relegated to the periphery of the academic enterprise and has become the least valued element in the traditional tenured faculty portfolio of teaching, research, and service. In some large research-oriented higher education institutions, contingent faculty teach the bulk of undergraduate courses, a trend that reflects the lower priority accorded to instruction, while a new generation of contingent junior scholars who are often women and faculty of color are assigned to teach these heavily enrolled introductory courses.[39]

For example, Nora, a white transgender disabled contingent faculty member in an eastern public research university, describes the tendency of chairs to assign lecturers to teach the large introductory sections, composed mostly of nonmajors. As she remarks, "I have to say I feel lucky; usually I get to teach the courses that I want to teach. That wasn't necessarily true with the chair; he very much pushed the lecturers to teach the intro level courses. . . . Lecturers are often hired with that in mind." Having taught the introductory course of over fifty students for many years, she underscores the challenges of teaching more controversial subject matter to nonmajors in these large undergraduate sections. "It's a very difficult class. It's not an easy subject to teach when you're teaching nonmajors who may have some level of resistance to these topics."

Significantly, the fragmentation of the faculty portfolio undermines student educational outcomes. For example, one of the benefits of student learning communities for low-income and first-generation students is precisely through a holistic approach that forges links across the curriculum and establishes connectivity between in-class and out-of-class experiences.[40] Further, consider the findings of a comprehensive study by Florence Ran and Di Xu of a state college system with two- and four-year institutions between the fall of 2005 and the summer of 2010. The study found that nontenured instruction was negatively associated with students' subsequent course enrollment in a given field of study. The largest negative effects derived from courses taught by short-term nontenured faculty. The researchers also found that instructor characteristics accounted for one quarter of the negative effects. In addition, it is notable that students received higher grades when taking courses with short-term nontenured faculty, lower grades in courses with long-term nontenured faculty, and the lowest grades with tenured faculty.[41]

THE INSURGENT WAVE OF ACADEMIC CAPITALISM

With the passage of time, the progressive trend toward neoliberalism and corporatization has evolved into what has been termed "academic capitalism." Since the 1970s, the neoliberal strain of academic capitalism has become more deeply embedded within the fabric and culture of higher education. As Sheila Slaughter and Gary Rhoades explain in their groundbreaking work *Academic Capitalism and the New Economy* (2004), universities have embraced more corporate-like and market-based activities that have brought the corporate sector within their walls and blurred the distinction between the private and public sectors. This development has fostered the emergence of "interstitial organizations" and created new networks of internal and external actors.[42] The forces of commodification and marketization have impacted institutional priorities, faculty work, and academic careers.[43] In this rapidly changing universe, the focus on efficiency and business-oriented operations emanating from centralized administration has led to faculty intellectual capital being viewed as a marketable product and revenue stream.[44]

The emphasis on revenue generation has become particularly pervasive in the science, technology, engineering, and mathematics (STEM) fields. Federalization of research through award of grants for research and development has altered the balance among fields and programs in research universities, with greater resources and status accorded to the STEM fields.[45] Scholars Amy Metcalf and Sheila Slaughter theorize that the shift from one prestige system (a traditional academic system with expert-based power) to another (an entrepreneurial system with market-based power) has allowed men to recapture historic privilege they had attained in higher education.[46] One could also argue that it has allowed majority males to recapture such privilege.

With the "valorizing" of research and pressures to obtain grant funding, Mark, a white male retired psychology professor from a private university, describes a growing generational divide in faculty expectations that has in turn resulted in negative treatment of talented senior faculty by their more junior counterparts:[47]

The reality was that in their era such funding was not expected or needed to do psychological research to the extent it is today. In the process, the senior faculty contributions to build programs with national reputations, create knowledge, and educate doctoral students and thousands of undergrads was cast aside and not acknowledged.

The trend toward privatization in public spaces has intruded into budgeting, curricula, and the educational process such as when scarce resources have promoted efforts to produce revenue through entrepreneurial activities Note the establishment of externally funded think tanks, foundations, and other entities on campus that have involved large donations from conservative entrepreneurs and dark money such as from the Charles Koch Foundation. These foundations are not neutral in orientation and actively seek to promote ideological perspectives among students. In many cases, the revenue sources of such intrusion into the academic and financial spheres are secret and unknown to students. Grassroots advocacy groups such as UnKoch My Campus and their campus-based affiliates have tried with some success to pressure universities to reveal the sources of donations to campus foundations and think tanks.

The founding of privately financed not-for-profit research foundations that serve as conservative think tanks on college campuses began as early as 1980 with the founding of the Center for Market Processes, later called the Mercatus Center, at George Mason University. Richard Fink, an economics professor, linked the center to Charles Koch, who served on the Mercatus board, and Brian Hooks, executive director of the Koch Foundation.[48] The center has provided support to selected graduate students mostly in economics and supplemented the salaries of some professors as well. While its mission is to bridge "the gap between academic ideas and real-world problems" through "market-oriented ideas,"[49] the Mercatus Center not only supports the training of students in its theories but also helps broaden the hidden network of ultraconservative institutes and associations focused on protecting capitalism from the perceived threat of social democratic forces.

CORPORATE VIEWS OF THE STUDENT AS CUSTOMER

An important manifestation of neoliberalism in higher education is the corporate-like emphasis on student as customer.[50] This trend has arisen as the ideological view of education has shifted from a public good to a private good, a perspective that is used to justify the large-scale under-funding of higher education. With efforts to attract students through marketing brochures, luxurious campus housing, and other amenities, the focus on student revenue has resulted in the commodification of campus attractions as a marketing strategy as reflected on many college websites.

In the realm of teaching, the contingent faculty model reinforces the role of student as customer through student evaluations that often play an important role in reemployment decisions. As a 2021 meta-analysis by Rebecca Kreitzman and Jennie Sweet-Cushner of over one hundred articles concludes, student evaluations of teaching are only weakly cor-related with learning. The study finds that women, faculty of color, and other marginalized groups are disadvantaged in student ratings. These researchers emphasize the need for studies of racial and intersectional identity bias because most of the equity bias research is focused on gen-der.[51] Other variables that can enter the process include age of the in-structor and the faculty member's political orientation.

A critical point reinforced in our interviews is that the tie of student evaluations to term-based reappointment can cause contingent faculty to try to please students, water down assignments, and inflate grades.[52] Treating students as customers refocuses the educational process on student satisfaction and redirects teaching toward delivering customer service, with the role of the teacher as entertainer rather than facilitator. The learning process itself then becomes an economic commodity, and students are oriented toward the value they receive for their money and for their specific needs rather than the educational experience itself.[53]

THE PREDOMINANCE OF ELITE WHITE MALE POWER STRUCTURES

Academic capitalism has opened the door to the significant expansion of administrative authority and reinforcement of the prevailing elite power dynamics dominated by white male actors in academe. The demograph-ics of top leadership in higher education reveal the continued domination of elite white males and the persistent lack of racial/ethnic and gender diversity in key administrative roles. Indeed, the profile of college presidents has remained virtually unchanged over three decades: the typical president is a white male in his early sixties, Protestant, and married with children. The lack of diversity also pertains to chief academic officers or provosts, who are usually the second-in-command and are also largely white and male, with nearly one-third over age sixty.[54] Similarly, a survey of 441 chief business officers (CBOs) conducted in 2021 reveals that the demographic composition of CBOs has not changed significantly over the last decade, with persisting racial and gender disparities. In fact, 87 percent of chief financial officers are white and 60 percent are male, while only 39 percent identify as female.[55] Further, the hiring of presidents from the corporate world and outside academe has in some prominent instances created significant disconnection with academic culture.

The lack of diversity in the upper echelons of higher education is significant, since the sites of power have shifted toward individuals in managerial and administrative roles who are involved in revenue generation.[56] In particular, the rising power and increasing influence of the CBO reflects the prominence of administrative authority and the prioritization of financial concerns in academic decision-making. With the mounting challenges posed by declining enrollment, decreases in state funding, rising tuition, and COVID-19, the sphere of influence of CBOs has expanded greatly. The influence of CBOs extends to the highest institutional levels, as they work in concert with the president and executive staff as well as with boards of trustees in staffing committees for finance, audit, and endowments/investments. Further, as the business functions of universities have expanded, more funds have been diverted away from the core educational enterprise.[57]

CBOs have an increasingly broad portfolio that typically includes budget and financial planning as well as overseeing controller duties and the bursar. More than three out of four (78 percent) of CBOs manage auxiliary services, and 71 percent work with investments and endowments. Half also have responsibility for internal audit public safety and internal audit. Other areas of oversight can include human resources, athletics, information technology, bookstores, facilities management, real estate, financial aid, and even legal affairs, admissions, research administration, and diversity offices.[58] Their responsibilities increasingly involve governmental relations such as working with legislatures and state governments. As can be seen from this data, CBOs wield considerable power in colleges and universities.

The influence of market-based forces in higher education is also evident in the trend toward the corporatization of boards of trustees and the appointment of trustees from the business world who may hold the majority on these boards. While financial and business experience does play a role in university management, these trustees are charged with overseeing academic decision-making, an area in which some have limited experience. As evidenced in a number of prominent instances, trustees can view college campuses as too liberal and not protective of conservative perspectives. The neoliberal value system of boards has been reflected in the emphasis on faculty productivity and institutional efficiency, often accompanied by a critical view of tenure.

Take, for example, the recent situation at the flagship University of North Carolina at Chapel Hill in which the university's conservative board of trustees did not approve tenure for Nikole Hannah-Jones, a Pulitzer Prize–winning journalist. Hannah-Jones had been appointed to the Knight Chair in Race and Investigative Journalism at the University of North Carolina Hussman School of Journalism, a position that conferred tenure to the last two incumbents. Despite the advocacy of Chancellor Kevin Guskiewicz before the board, the board that is made up of ten white males did not vote on her tenure bid, effectively denying her tenure. She was ultimately offered a five-year appointment.

Conservatives were clearly concerned about Hannah-Jones's work on the *New York Times Magazine*'s 1619 project that explored the history of slavery in the United States.[59] A group of thirty-six journalism professors at the University of North Carolina at Chapel Hill filed an open letter to the board of trustees describing the trustee's "blatant disregard for time-honored tenure procedures and for the university and Board of Trustees' endorsed values of diversity, equity, and inclusion."[60] Jelani Cobb, professor of journalism at Columbia University, described the board's action as a "blatant intrusion of politics into what is supposed to be protected by academic freedom."[61] In response to the board's action, Hannah-Jones and a team of attorneys from the NAACP Legal Defense Fund informed the university that they were considering filing a discrimination lawsuit.[62] Her letter referred to "political interference and influence from a powerful donor," later identified as Walter E. Hussman Jr., an Arkansas newspaper publisher for whom the journalism school is named who has pledged $25 million to the school. But after extreme public pressure and the support of the Robert Wood Johnson Foundation, a major university donor, the board held a special meeting and in a vote of 9–4 finally approved tenure for Hannah-Jones.[63] The substantial Republican pushback against the 1619 Project resulted in the filing of bills in a number of state legislatures designed to cut funding to K–12 schools and colleges that provide classes on the project.

CORPORATE CONSULTING AND TOOLS OF THE ADMINISTRATIVE BUREAUCRACY

As colleges and universities have faced serious budget constraints, one of the major tools employed to address programmatic cuts is the hiring of corporate consultants to deliver difficult news. These consulting firms receive substantial fees for recommending areas to cut and are used to bolster the administrative decision-making process. Take the hiring of Huron Consulting by a large set of universities including the University of Wisconsin, the University of New Hampshire, and the New School for Social Research. Huron Consulting was founded by twenty-five members of the Arthur Andersen Consulting Firm, which had been involved in financial fraud in its work with Enron and was fined millions of dollars in 2009 for overstating pretax income.[64] The firm's standard recommendations for cost cutting include faculty and staff layoffs, salary reductions, hiring freezes, outsourcing of staff functions, and program closures. The typical business model that Huron has employed in higher education since its entry into the field in 2015 seems to reflect what critics call "textbook neoliberalism" and is reminiscent of Naomi Klein's description of "shock doctrine" tactics in which neoliberal actors use crises to implement radical, corporatized measures.[65]

A case in point is Huron Consulting's role in the budget-cutting process at the New School for Social Research in New York City, a progressive institution with liberal ideals. A new president, Dwight A. McBride, an African American male, was hired on March 16, 2020, in the midst of the pandemic. Facing a potential budget deficit of $130 million in the 2020 fiscal year, McBride hired Huron at an undisclosed cost to conduct a "reimagining project." In its cost-cutting initiative, the school drew down $80 million from its endowment, almost a quarter of its total value.[66] Five months later in August 2020, the school laid off 122 employees, or 13 percent of its administrative staff, most of whom were lower-level staff. In addition, employees who had been furloughed in March were not recalled.

The New School's layoffs of lower-level staff at the height of the pandemic drew vigorous community protests and was in clear contrast with the average compensation of $430,000 paid to the New School's top twenty-five leaders in 2018.[67] Analysis of compensation data by Sanjay Reddy, an economics professor at the school, found that the president made more in 2017 than the president of Harvard in proportion to the school's endowment. Between 2014 and 2019, management salaries increased 45 percent while revenue only grew by 17 percent.[68] But the aggregate administrative layoffs of roughly two hundred employees from the payroll and health insurance rolls were estimated to only result in $5 million for the 2020 fiscal year and $12 million in 2021–2022.[69]

Emerson Brathwaite, an assistant in the drama department and the only person of color in drama administration, described his feeling of being discarded when he was laid off. "How do you guys preach EDI [equity, diversity, and inclusion] and you release the only person of color you have on your staff?" Critics assailed President McBride's seven-figure salary even though he took a 15 percent cut and raised concerns about the $15 million townhouse owned by the school as well as the construction of a university center involving long-term debt of $595 million.[70]

In another example, a "reimagining" assessment by Huron Consulting was begun at the University of New Hampshire in 2019 at a cost of $600,000. The project was designed to save $12 million over two years.[71] In the spring of 2020, President James W. Dean Jr. shared his anticipation that there would be a reduction in the number of full-time equivalencies based on the results of the implementation teams.[72] The report generated by Huron, "Executive Summary of Resource Assessment and Academic Program Cost," highlighted nine "business case opportunities" designed to yield bottom-line improvement and was couched in language drawn from the corporate sector. One aspect of the analysis was directed toward academic cost management based on data pertaining to credit hour production and distribution. In reviewing academic program costs, the report focused specifically on efficiencies and market demand including such measures as student employability without addressing student learning outcomes or qualitative factors in the educational experience.[73] These market-oriented templates imposed on the academic landscape seem to reflect the unquestioned blurring of corporate and academic sectors, with the ascendancy of market-oriented quantitative factors. Not surprisingly, the creation of the new position of chief marketing officer was announced by the president in June 2021.

A prominent administratively oriented instrument for downsizing academic programs in higher education is academic program review. Presidents and provosts may initiate such review due to budgetary constraints or even when other factors such as pressures from boards or calls for efficiency are the driving force.[74] Such assessments often lean heavily toward quantitative measures such as enrollment, number of majors, and cost per credit hour without a corresponding emphasis on qualitative data. They can be couched in neoliberal, corporatized language of "quality assurance" and "external accountability," with repeated references in one assessment guide, for example, to "the industry of higher education."[75]

The consequences of academic program review can be severe and result in the closure of departments and layoff of tenured faculty. Unsurprisingly, academic politics can enter the program review process and can generate backlash. For example, if some faculty are involved in the prioritization process, they can face alienation from colleagues for their role in recommending program cuts. As one faculty member at St. Joseph's College in New York City and Long Island put it during the process of academic program review during 2016, it felt like "classic antiworker practice." He added, "They basically want us to put the nails on our own coffins. I don't think anything we write in these reports is going to make for a different outcome. They just want us to go through the motions and stay docile and busy."[76]

CONCLUSION

With the unremitting advance of legislative cutbacks in state funding, many institutions of higher education have had to resort to layoffs of both contingent and tenured faculty or even close their doors permanently. In this chapter, we have shared recent research findings that illuminate the link between the decline of state funding for public higher education by conservative legislatures and increasing student diversity.

At the same time, with the advent of neoliberalism, academic capitalism has taken hold within administrative infrastructures in higher education. These tendencies are reflected in increased corporate influence and a corresponding privileging of external funding. Clear evidence of corporatization can be seen in the composition of boards of trustees, the hiring of expensive consultants, and the selection of presidents at some institutions from the corporate world or of individuals without terminal academic degrees.

With the now prevalent contingent faculty model, teaching has been unbundled from the traditional tenured faculty triumvirate of teaching, research, and service. This unbundling has in turn led to a devaluation of teaching itself, accompanied by the rapid expansion of the ranks of contingent faculty who occupy a significantly lower echelon in the academic hierarchy. The disparate pay, working conditions, and lack of health care for many contingent faculty have created a vast inequity in the academic workforce. This disparity is heightened by the creation of near at-will status for much of the contingent faculty cohort, a pattern that replicates administrative appointments. These factors have encroached rapidly on academic freedom and facilitated significantly greater administrative control of the faculty workforce.

To provide further context for the study, in the next chapter we share an overview of the demographics of contingent faculty in four-year institutions. Through this more detailed analysis, we seek to obtain a clearer picture of trends and patterns in contingent faculty employment, particularly with regard to the representation of women and faculty of color.

2

Demographics of the New Academic Underclass

Overreliance on contingent appointments, which
lack the protection of tenure for academic freedom
and the economic security of continuing appointments,
threatens the success of institutions in fulfilling
their obligations to students and to society.
GLENN COLBY, *DATA SNAPSHOT: TENURE AND*
CONTINGENCY IN US HIGHER EDUCATION

We now highlight major demographic trends in the unrelenting growth of the contingent faculty employment model in four-year institutions over a period of five decades coupled with the progressive erosion of tenure-line positions. The data shared in this chapter illuminate the disempowerment of the faculty role through the imposition of contingent faculty workforce models. This large-scale restructuring clearly reflects the impact of neoliberal trends, political partisanship, and decreased funding on the rapid expansion of the contingent faculty ranks. As a proviso to this analysis, it is important to note that the historical data on the decline of tenure-line faculty is complex, nuanced, and subject to changes in the survey methodology and the availability of data. As a result, different analysts have drawn substantially different conclusions from the data. Since our focus is on four-year colleges and universities, the data we share is limited to this broad category and may not reflect the realities in two-year institutions. We have, however, included in our analysis associate degree institutions that offer baccalaureate degrees.

Although the hiring of adjunct faculty was historically more prevalent at community colleges, the majority of contingent faculty are now employed at four-year institutions.[1] Further, the largest growth in adjuncts across all sectors has occurred at doctoral institutions. This troubling development has implications for scholarship and research and is coupled with a decline in tenure-line positions. Table 2.1 (see pp. 52–53) depicts the distribution of adjuncts across all sectors as of 2019.

As tenured faculty retire, their permanent positions are increasingly replaced with contingent lines.[2] A study of contingent faculty over the twenty-year time span from 1993–1994 to 2013–2014 also found that the most significant growth was in public institutions, with twice the growth compared to private institutions.[3] These figures are correlated with the progressive decline in state funding for higher education.

THE DECLINE OF TENURED FACULTY POSITIONS

Let us take a closer look at the dimensions of the reconfiguration of the faculty workforce over the past half century. Consider the startling fact that in 1969, 78.3 percent of faculty members at colleges and universities held full-time, tenured, and tenure-track positions, with only 21.7 positions in part-time contingent lines. By 2009 this ratio had flipped. Tenure-line faculty had decreased to 33.5 percent of faculty appointments, with 66.5 percent in contingent appointments.[4] Table 2.2 (see p. 54) depicts the unrelenting increase in the percentage of part-time faculty since 1970 in both four-year and two-year institutions. For example, one empirical study identified a 114.5 percent increase in the number of part-time faculty between 1993 and 2013 and an 87 percent increase in full-time contingent faculty during this period, while the number of full-time faculty only increased by 31.3 percent.[5]

Nonetheless, in interpreting this historical data, Phillip Magness, conservative critic and academic program director at the Charles Koch–linked Institute for Humane Studies at George Mason University, posits that the decrease in the percentage of full-time faculty is misleading. He notes that percentages do not portray the substantial increase in the number of full-time positions coupled with the much more rapid expansion in the number of part-time adjunct positions. In other words, the actual number of full-time faculty has increased over the years, while adjunct positions have expanded even more rapidly.[6]

While Magness's interpretation may be true in terms of sheer numbers, the statistics on full-time faculty offered in support of this theory replicate those in table 2.2 (p. 54) and include both contingent and tenure-line positions. By pooling all full-time positions together, this analysis does not reflect the diminishing numbers of tenure-line positions or what we know to be the corresponding increase in the full-time contingent cohort. Further, Magness and his colleague Jason Brennan at Georgetown University insist that adjuncts are *"supplementing*, not *replacing*," full-time faculty. As they state, "adjunct growth is largely supplemental to a stable and growing full-time faculty base that has historically kept pace with student enrollment."[7] Once again, note that these figures include contingent full-time faculty.

Counteracting this perspective, consider the fact that between 2000 and 2019, tenure-line faculty at four-year and not-for-profit institutions only increased 12 percent in comparison to an increase of 27 percent in student enrollment.[8] Similarly, an extensive research study by Martin Finkelstein, Valerie Conley, and Jack Schuster finds that the proportion of full-time tenured or tenure-track faculty shrank from 43.6 percent in 1993 to 29.7 percent in 2013. They describe the fluid educational environment in which the faculty model has been "abruptly restructured and repurposed in recent years" as a radical redistribution from traditional tenure-line appointments through a centrifugal effect that has resulted in the expansion of contingent positions. Further, these scholars indicate that the redeployment of faculty that has occurred over a significant time period has accelerated and expanded in terms of the diverse types of non-tenure-track appointments. In their view, we have now reached a tipping point in higher education where no reversal of this redistribution is in evidence.[9]

Brennan and Magness further surmise that the recent wave of adjunct positions over the last two decades is a result of the for-profit higher education industry and "its vastly disproportionate use of adjunct faculty." They indicate with the proliferation of not-for-profit colleges and universities between 1990 and 2011, fully one quarter of the increase in adjunct appointments can be attributed to this boom.[10] Yet, in our sample of four-year institutions we find that as of 2019, a larger share of adjuncts are employed on average at not-for-profit public and private colleges and universities. As shown in table 2.1 (pp. 52–53), the average number of adjuncts per institution at private not-for-profit four-year institutions is 288, roughly double the average number or 134 at private for-profit institutions.

These researchers also dispute the view of adjunct employment as exploitation. In a controversial article titled "Are Adjunct Faculty Exploited? Some Grounds for Skepticism," they assert that unlike so-called sweatshop workers, the majority of adjuncts do not hold PhDs. But the data they cite is based on a 2003–2004 sample survey from the National Study of Postsecondary Faculty that was discontinued.[11] As a result, there is no equivalent existing or current data source to determine the accuracy of their statement regarding terminal degrees held by adjuncts. Remarkably, Brennan and Magness further assert that "adjunct faculty, unlike sweatshop workers, are in a large degree responsible for putting themselves in a bad situation."[12] They add without any supporting evidence, "in general, adjunct faculty, unlike sweatshop workers, have good exit options—they are not stuck being adjuncts, and could instead secure well-paying white collar jobs." This shocking argument places the blame on adjunct faculty themselves for the prevailing institutional hierarchy and the system of two-tiered faculty employment. In a powerful counterpoint, Mark Purcell, professor at the University of Washington, writes,

> They [contingent faculty] are therefore in the position of being expected to feel lucky when they feel deeply unlucky. They understand, far better than most tenure-track faculty, how decidedly arbitrary hiring decisions are, how entry into the tenure stream is far more a matter of good fortune than good work. They know their limbo is the result of not yet having matched perfectly an available tenure-track job. Yet they get continual messages that their limbo is self-imposed, the result of their own failings, and so they should feel lucky and grateful for their non-tenure-track position.[13]

Put simply, Brennan and Magness ignore the sweeping tide of neoliberalism and corporatized administrative financial practices that have led to a monumental shift in faculty employment. Instead they places the blame on individual non-tenure-track faculty for their current employment status.

OVERALL TRENDS

Moving forward, we do note some distinctions within institutional types in terms of the percentage of full-time and part-time contingent faculty employed. These differences are critical to understanding the context for contingent faculty workplace practices. Table 2.3 (see p. 55) and figure 2.1 (see p. 56) reveal that associate's colleges with four-year degrees employ a larger percentage of the contingent workforce in part-time adjunct positions (81.4 percent), compared to doctoral institutions that employ a larger portion of the contingent workforce in the more secure full-time positions (42.1 percent).

In terms of race/ethnicity as shown in tables 2.4, 2.5, 2.6, and 2.7 (see pp. 57–60), as of 2019 nearly one quarter of part- and full-time contingent faculty in four-year institutions were people of color.[14] While Black and African American incumbents held 8.8 percent of adjunct positions in 2019, they only held 6.4 percent of the more stable full-time contingent positions. Asian American incumbents held 5.6 percent of adjunct positions and a larger share (10.1 percent) of full-time contingent jobs. Interestingly, special four-year institutions that include professional schools of engineering, business, law, business, and arts/music employ the most diverse cohort of adjuncts (30.6 percent). These representational statistics are roughly parallel to the tenured faculty workforce and reflect the need for increased diversification across all faculty lines. A number of our interviewees for this study expressly identified the lack of diversity among contingent faculty in their institutions and identified the parallel between the lack of diverse faculty role models in both tenured and contingent ranks.

The feminization of the adjunct workforce is another noticeable trend, with women holding a slightly smaller share of full-time contingent positions. Between 1993 and 2013, women's part-time faculty appointments increased from 48.2 percent to 56.1 percent, while their full-time appointments decreased from 64.5 percent to 55.7 percent.[15] In 2019, women held 54.1 percent of nearly 419,000 adjunct positions in 2,780 four-year institutions compared to 45.8 percent held by men. But most note that the more secure full-time positions were held by men, with 51.6 percent of the 205,456 contingent positions in 2,549 institutions compared to 48.4 percent for women.[16]

From a generational standpoint, a survey of 502 adjuncts in 2018 found that approximately 70 percent of adjuncts are over age 40 and that the average age is 50.[17] As a result, the intersectionality of demographic characteristics of adjuncts and contingent faculty not only involves race/ethnicity, gender, and sexual orientation but also has ramifications in terms of age and generational status. For example, as women age in the adjunct ranks, they can be passed over for newly minted scholars from more recent generations for tenured appointments. As Angela Fulk, a longtime adjunct faculty member, explains, "Once in that ghettoized space, most of us will find it impossible to escape." She describes the bias against adjuncts that makes it difficult to advance professionally, since some assume that the failure of adjuncts to attain permanent employment is due to some error or weakness on their part.[18]

CONCLUSION

The demographic analysis shared in this chapter offers a clear picture of the representation of minoritized faculty in contingent roles in four-year institutions as well as the relative distribution of appointment types across these institutions. Overall, the data reveal that there has been a continuous decimation of tenure track and tenured faculty lines over the last half century coupled with a proliferation of contingent positions. While elite universities have been somewhat slower in the adoption of contingent positions, the new norm of a two-tiered faculty model is deeply ensconced within the fabric of higher education as a whole. The data also reveal a rough comparability in the ratio of minoritized faculty in both tenure-line positions and contingent faculty ranks. Clearly, the representation of diverse contingent and tenured faculty has not kept pace with the increasing diversification of the student body. But at the same time, larger numbers of women are assuming contingent positions in an increasing feminization of this workforce.

As we have noted, the contingent employment model offers significant administrative convenience and cost savings to institutions, regardless of the impact on student learning and the exigencies of the non-tenure-track faculty experience. Given this demographic overview, we move forward in the next chapter to explore the first-person narratives of minoritized contingent faculty and highlight common themes that characterize their experiences in academe.

TABLE 2.1 Adjunct faculty by sector (public, private for-profit, private not-for-profit) and institutional type

	PUBLIC	PRIVATE NOT-FOR-PROFIT	PRIVATE FOR-PROFIT	TOTAL
SPECIAL 4-YEAR	7,448	31,141	12,287	50,876
ASSOCIATE'S COLLEGES WITH 4-YEAR DEGREES	36,016	1,804	3,349	41,169
BACCALAUREATE	7,967	21,392	2,094	31,453
MASTER'S	60,846	71,493	8,611	140,950
DOCTORAL	92,832	73,746	14,573	181,151
TOTAL NO. OF ADJUNCTS	205,109	199,576	40,914	445,599
NO. OF INSTITUTIONS	711	1,485	278	2,474

	SPECIAL 4-YEAR	ASSOCIATE COLLEGES WITH 4-YEAR DEGREES	BACCALAUREATE	MASTER'S	DOCTORAL	TOTAL
PUBLIC	7,448	36,016	7,967	60,846	92,832	205,109
PRIVATE NOT-FOR-PROFIT	31,141	1,804	21,392	71,493	73,746	199,576
PRIVATE FOR-PROFIT	12,287	3,349	2,094	8,611	14,573	40,914
TOTAL NO. OF ADJUNCTS	50,876	41,169	31,453	140,950	181,151	445,599
NO. OF INSTITUTIONS	727	212	481	649	405	2,474

	NO. OF INSTITUTIONS
SPECIAL 4-YEAR	727
ASSOCIATE'S COLLEGES WITH 4-YEAR DEGREES	212
BACCALAUREATE	481
MASTER'S	649
DOCTORAL	405
TOTAL	2,474

Source: Integrated Postsecondary Education Data System, Spring 2019. Analysis by authors.

TABLE 2.2 Ratio of full-time and part-time faculty (all institutional types), 1970–2018*

| YEAR | TOTAL | EMPLOYMENT STATUS | | | |
		FULL-TIME	PART-TIME	% FULL-TIME	% FEMALE
1970	474,000	369,000	104,000	77.8	—
1975	628,000	440,000	188,000	70.1	—
1980	686,000	450,000	236,000	65.6	—
1985	715,000	459,000	256,000	64.2	—
1991	826,252	535,623	290,629	64.8	36.4
1995	931,706	550,822	380,884	59.1	39.6
2001	1,113,183	617,868	495,315	55.5	42.1
2005	1,290,426	675,624	614,802	52.4	44.6
2011	1,524,469	762,114	762,355	50.0	48.2
2016	1,546,081	813,978	732,103	52.6	49.3
2018	1,542,613	832,119	710,494	53.9	50.0

Source: US Department of Education, *Digest of Education Statistics, 2020*, Table 315.10.
*Data prior to 1987 are based on enrollment estimates and data after 1995 reflect a change in the methodology from institutions of higher education to degree-granting institutions that include more community colleges.

TABLE 2.3 Full-time and part-time contingent faculty by institutional type (excludes unknown, nonresident)

	SPECIAL 4-YEAR		ASSOCIATE'S COLLEGES WITH 4-YEAR DEGREES		BACCALAUREATE		MASTER'S		DOCTORAL	
	FT	PT	FT	PT	FT	PT	FT	PT	FT	PT
NO.	34,507	45,760	7,427	32,504	13,058	28,049	38,761	138,290	130,550	179,394
%	43.0	57.0	18.6	81.4	31.8	68.2	31.8	68.2	42.1	57.9

	NO. OF INSTITUTIONS
SPECIAL 4-YEAR	513
ASSOCIATE'S COLLEGES WITH 4-YEAR DEGREES	172
BACCALAUREATE	451
MASTER'S	632
DOCTORAL	400
TOTAL	2,168

Source: Integrated Postsecondary Education Data System, Spring 2019. Analysis by authors.

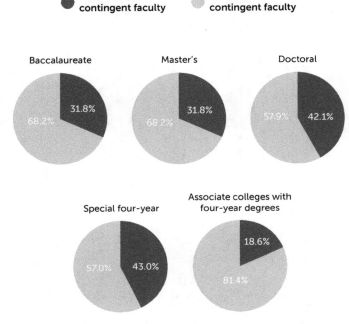

FIGURE 2.1 Relative distribution of part- and full-time contingent faculty appointments by institutional type. (Source: Integrated Postsecondary Education Data System, Spring 2019. Analysis by authors.)

TABLE 2.4 Adjunct faculty by consolidated race/ethnicity and gender by institutional type (excludes unknown, nonresident)

RACE/ETHNICITY	GENDER	SPECIAL 4-YEAR (%)	ASSOCIATE'S COLLEGES WITH 4-YEAR DEGREES (%)	BACCALAUREATE (%)	MASTER'S (%)	DOCTORAL (%)	TOTAL (%)
BIPOC*	Male	13.0	9.9	9.7	9.8	9.5	10.0
	Female	17.6	13.6	12.9	13.5	13.3	13.7
White	Male	34.5	35.7	35.9	34.6	37.0	35.7
	Female	34.9	40.8	41.5	42.1	40.2	40.6
	Total (%)	100.0	100.0	100.0	100.0	100.00	100.00

	NO. OF INSTITUTIONS
SPECIAL 4-YEAR	727
ASSOCIATE'S COLLEGES WITH 4-YEAR DEGREES	212
BACCALAUREATE	481
MASTER'S	649
DOCTORAL	405
TOTAL	2,474

Source: Integrated Postsecondary Education Data System, Spring 2019. Analysis by authors.
*Black, Indigenous, and People of Color.

TABLE 2.5 Adjunct faculty by race/ethnicity and gender by institutional type (excludes unknown, nonresident)

RACE/ETHNICITY	GENDER	SPECIAL 4-YEAR (%)	ASSOCIATE'S COLLEGES WITH 4-YEAR DEGREES (%)	BACCALAUREATE (%)	MASTER'S (%)	DOCTORAL (%)	TOTAL (%)
American Indian or Alaskan Native	Male	0.2	0.2	0.2	0.2	0.2	0.2
	Female	0.2	0.3	0.3	0.3	0.2	0.3
Asian	Male	4.4	2.4	1.4	2.2	3.0	2.6
	Female	5.0	2.8	2.0	2.5	3.4	3.0
Black or African American	Male	3.3	3.3	3.8	3.6	2.7	3.2
	Female	6.3	5.6	5.8	5.9	5.2	5.6
Hispanic or Latino	Male	4.4	3.4	3.6	3.1	3.0	3.3
	Female	5.0	4.0	4.0	3.9	3.6	3.9
Native Hawaiian or other Pacific Islander	Male	0.1	0.1	0.2	0.1	0.1	0.1
	Female	0.2	0.1	0.2	0.1	0.1	0.1
Two or more races	Male	0.6	0.5	0.4	0.5	0.5	0.5
	Female	0.9	0.8	0.6	0.8	0.8	0.8
White	Male	34.5	35.6	35.9	34.6	37.0	35.7
	Female	34.9	40.8	41.5	42.1	40.2	40.6
Total (%)		100.0	100.0	100.0	100.0	100.0	100.0

Source: Integrated Postsecondary Education Data System, Spring 2019. Analysis by authors.

TABLE 2.6 Full-time contingent faculty by consolidated race/ethnicity and gender and contract type

RACE/ETHNICITY	GENDER	SPECIAL 4-YEAR			ASSOCIATE'S COLLEGES WITH 4-YEAR DEGREES			BACCALAUREATE			MASTER'S			DOCTORAL			TOTAL (%)
		MULTIYEAR (%)	ANNUAL CONTRACT (%)	LESS THAN ANNUAL CONTRACT (%)	MULTIYEAR (%)	ANNUAL CONTRACT (%)	LESS THAN ANNUAL CONTRACT (%)	MULTIYEAR (%)	ANNUAL CONTRACT (%)	LESS THAN ANNUAL CONTRACT (%)	MULTIYEAR (%)	ANNUAL CONTRACT (%)	LESS THAN ANNUAL CONTRACT (%)	MULTIYEAR (%)	ANNUAL CONTRACT (%)	LESS THAN ANNUAL CONTRACT (%)	
BIPOC*	Male	13.1	15.4	11.9	8.5	12.9	21.1	7.0	11.1	16.8	8.7	8.2	12.0	10.9	9.9	10.3	10.7
	Female	16.4	18.5	15.8	10.6	11.6	24.3	9.9	13.8	21.0	12.3	11.8	16.9	13.4	13.1	13.9	13.7
White	Male	35.1	34.9	34.3	44.2	39.1	31.3	44.1	39.3	29.7	44.4	46.3	40.7	39.8	42.0	44.4	40.8
	Female	35.5	31.2	38.0	36.7	36.4	23.4	39.1	35.9	32.5	34.6	33.8	30.4	35.8	35.0	31.4	34.8
Total (%)		100.0	100.0	100.0	100.0	100.0	100.0	100.0	100.0	100.0	100.0	100.0	100.0	100.0	100.0	100.0	100.0

Source: Integrated Postsecondary Education Data System, Spring 2019. Analysis by authors.

*Black, Indigenous, and People of Color.

TABLE 2.7 Full-time contingent faculty by race/ethnicity and gender by institutional type (excludes unknown, nonresident)

RACE/ETHNICITY	GENDER	SPECIAL 4-YEAR (%)	ASSOCIATE'S COLLEGES WITH 4-YEAR DEGREES (%)	BACCALAUREATE (%)	MASTER'S (%)	DOCTORAL (%)	TOTAL (%)
American Indian or Alaskan Native	Male	0.1	0.3	0.2	0.2	0.1	0.1
	Female	0.2	0.3	0.3	0.3	0.2	0.2
Asian	Male	8.0	1.9	2.2	2.2	5.2	4.9
	Female	8.1	1.8	2.9	2.6	5.6	5.2
Black or African American	Male	2.3	2.5	4.0	3.1	1.9	2.3
	Female	4.5	3.4	5.3	5.2	3.3	3.9
Hispanic or Latino	Male	3.3	6.7	2.9	2.4	2.6	2.8
	Female	4.0	5.9	3.5	3.2	3.4	3.6
Native Hawaiian or other specific Islander	Male	0.1	0.3	0.2	0.1	0.1	0.1
	Female	0.1	0.4	0.1	0.1	0.1	0.1
Two or more races	Male	0.5	0.5	0.5	0.6	0.4	0.5
	Female	0.7	0.7	0.6	0.9	0.7	0.7
White	Male	35.0	40.1	40.5	45.2	41.1	40.8
	Female	33.1	35.3	36.9	34.0	35.2	34.8
Total (%)		100.0	100.0	100.0	100.0	100.0	100.0

Source: Integrated Postsecondary Education Data System, Spring 2019. Analysis by authors.

3

The Precarious Working Conditions of Minoritized Contingent Faculty

---

Adjuncts are higher education's version of migrant laborers—professionals hopping from campus to campus with no job security, a meager income, no health insurance or retirement benefits, and little hope for advancement.

MARK DROZDOWSKI, "THE PLIGHT OF ADJUNCT FACULTY ON AMERICA'S CAMPUSES"

I n this chapter, we share the personal narratives of contingent faculty members in four-year institutions and identify the major themes that emerged from our interviews. The frank and searing accounts of these faculty illuminate the ways in which structural power imbalances, unstable working conditions, and minoritized status affect their day-to-day work experiences. Because of the pent-up stress resulting from the perilous conditions of employment, several faculty mentioned that the interviews were, in a sense, cathartic by giving them space to express their concerns and frustrations. Yet, despite the barriers they have faced and continue to face in their own academic careers, these contingent faculty expressed deep commitment to their students and to the integrity of the educational process. From this standpoint, relatively few issues were mentioned in relation to the classroom. Most concerns focused on their tenuous employment status and marginalization within the halls of academe.

The predominant themes identified in our interviews focus on the following six areas:

1. Isolation and exclusion in predominantly white institutions;
2. Stress arising from differential performance expectations and the need to work harder in order to prove one's worth;
3. Heavy teaching loads and inadequate compensation with little time for independent research;
4. Lack of input into academic decision-making such as in curricular matters, course assignments, and pedagogical methods;
5. Overreliance by department chairs and program directors on student evaluations that can reflect bias toward women and people of color; and
6. Limited ability to participate in shared governance.

Ironically, these themes largely coincide with the stress-producing circumstances identified over thirty-five years ago by Judith Gappa, a leading advocate for reform of part-time faculty employment. Gappa noted six stress-producing factors that affect all aspects of part-time employment: secondary employment status, job insecurity, lack of participation in decision-making, inadequate compensation, last preference in assignments and course load, and inadequate performance evaluation.[1] Although not specifically mentioned in Gappa's analysis, we add minoritized status as a major category in this assessment of stress-producing factors. And strikingly, the working conditions for contingent faculty have not improved over time. The lack of attention to working conditions of contingent faculty by institutions of higher education over a period of decades remains a major issue.

As indicated earlier, double marginalization occurs through the structure of contingent employment coupled with the exclusion that can result from holding minoritized social identities. Our interviews reveal substantial pain, stress, and anxiety for minoritized individuals resulting from exclusionary work experiences that often exact a substantial psychological, cognitive, and emotional toll. Further, when faced with differential treatment, these individuals may have difficulty in trying to decode ambiguous behaviors. In a climate of uncertainty, they may not be able to determine what steps to take to avert such situations in the future. At least two of the incidents described by minoritized contingent faculty in this chapter involve clear violation of accepted human resource practices and even legal requirements. Other incidents reflect the escalation of student complaints without apparent merit to the highest university levels, causing continuous stress fear of nonrenewal for the affected faculty.

On a larger scale, contingency represents the apocryphal canary in the coal mine, in this case an early warning signal of the damage resulting from the dissipation of the traditional educational model. The predominance of contingent faculty employment is a precursor of a decline in educational quality resulting from the wholesale commodification of the educational process. The emphasis of many institutions on boosting enrollment numbers and college rankings, marketing campus amenities, and lining budgetary coffers has led to a production-like focus on filling seats and subsequently staffing courses through last-minute decisions. Clearly, the preeminence of the bottom line has prevailed in the context of a steep decrease in state funding for public higher education. But at the same time, budgetary dollars often appear mysteriously available for purposes outside of teaching such as executive salaries, athletics, and other desired undertakings.

Building on our earlier analysis, the regressive treatment of contingent faculty as a secondary labor pool reinforces the neoliberal scaffolding inherent in academic capitalism. In a tightening economy in which few tenure-track job opportunities exist, individuals with doctoral degrees have been forced to take limited-term teaching appointments out of sheer economic necessity. Contrary to the picture of adjuncts as individuals who typically do not hold terminal degrees painted by Brennan and Magness in their research,[2] almost all the part- and full-time contingent faculty we interviewed do hold PhDs, and their degrees are often from elite public and private doctoral research universities. In fact, at some institutions holding a PhD is a threshold expectation for the appointment of contingent faculty. Yet, while the individuals we interviewed hold impressive academic credentials, they have had to compete in a market glutted with recent doctoral recipients. The inexorable forces of market supply and demand have driven the terms and conditions of their employment.

ISOLATION IN PREDOMINANTLY WHITE INSTITUTIONS

Many of the minoritized faculty we interviewed described their isolation in predominantly white institutions. Often they are among the few faculty from nondominant groups, both tenured and contingent, in their departments or schools. And as shown in an extensive body of research literature over more than three decades, such solo minoritized status can lead to tokenism, perceptions of incompetence, extreme and exaggerated evaluations, attribution to being an affirmative action hire, and biased stereotyping.[3] In this regard, consider how LeeAnn, an African American administrator and contingent faculty member in a private eastern university, describes the difficulty of becoming part of a community in a predominantly white institution:

> I think when you're an adjunct, or a contingent faculty member, it is very difficult and challenging to find your place in the community. . . . I think it's difficult enough to find my community, a community of African American faculty and staff as a full-time person.

Viviana, a Southeast Asian female adjunct faculty member at an elite private university, describes her hiring in terms of explicit diversity goals:

I think, honestly, the reason I was brought on is because I look different than the majority of sort of old white men who teach here. . . . And
I think they were very clear. . . . And the person who invited me said,
"Frankly, I really would like somebody who's a woman and who's not
white and who's deeply embedded in the field as a practitioner. You
combine those things to teach the course that you design." So, I think
it was pretty explicit that they were looking to diversify their faculty.

Once hired, as is well documented throughout the diversity literature,
some minoritized non-tenure-track faculty, like their tenured counterparts, experience cultural taxation. They are called upon to serve on diversity initiatives in other schools on their campuses or to represent their
racial/ethnic group on committees. They may be asked to advise minoritized students or undertake other forms of uncompensated service.[4]
David, a Latino male faculty member in a southwestern public research
university, describes this phenomenon in predominantly white institutions with limited numbers of diverse faculty:

I think part of it is that we don't have a large group of faculty of color
to draw from. So, you end up doing a lot more duty work as a faculty
of color. . . . [I]nitially a lot of the offers that I was getting to work
on panels and service capacity was as a Latino. It was like we want
you to come in because you are Latino or because a student mentioned that you were first generation. . . . So, I was getting opportunities, not necessarily because they thought I was really qualified or
because they thought I was going to be a huge asset to them, but because they thought, "we need this perspective so we're just going to
go get that person."

Further, the geographic location of campuses in largely white towns and
rural areas can exacerbate the marginalization and isolation of minoritized faculty. For example, Julie, a full-time contingent biracial faculty

member in an eastern doctoral research university located in a largely white rural area, explains how her actions are subject to intense scrutiny in this isolated environment. Note how she emphasizes that if she does something well it is ignored, but if she makes a single mistake she does not receive the benefit of the doubt her white colleagues receive:

> In class with my students, I'm very conscious that I'm in a very non-diverse place; the dynamic I have to prove [is] that I earned my class. If I make one mistake, I don't get the benefit of the doubt my white colleagues would get. If I do everything perfect and great, it doesn't matter.

Due to her low nine-month salary, Julie is not able to live in the college town where the university is located because of a lack of affordable housing. The only place where she can afford to live is in a small town close to the university that lacks the rich cultural life and availability of public transportation of the university town. And there are no buses from the small town to the university during the summer or even during the weekends when school is in session. In fact, there are no routes anywhere outside the university. As a result, Julie views the university as unresponsive to the need for public transportation in this rural environment and even sees willfulness in the failure to provide university busses. As she states, "the administration took advantage of the pandemic to cut back the bus routes and even had a plan to discard them completely."

Julie indicates that the circumstances relating to the university's isolated location has led to a revolving door for faculty of color. To further add to her sense of isolation in the community, Julie has been exposed to racist treatment when simply taking a walk with a Black colleague. This treatment intensified after the attack by a violent mob of supporters of former president Donald Trump on the US Capitol on January 6, 2021:

> I am treated differently here too. Do you realize that diversity doesn't want to come here? Half of the population is very racist. After the

January 6 insurrection, I didn't leave my apartment for two weeks. Trucks slow down next to us to stare at us every single time I went for a walk with my friend who is Black. There is no community outside of work. You don't pay me enough. I have to live in this small town, where I feel unwelcome just because of the way I look and where I have to tiptoe and not go to certain areas.

We will discuss the implications of the January 6 attack on the Capitol for minoritized faculty further in chapter 5. Julie's narrative underscores how the working conditions and lack of support for minoritized faculty in isolated geographic environments have ripple effects both within and outside the university community.

DIFFERENTIAL TREATMENT AND STRESS

As we have emphasized, the very nature of part- and full-time contingent faculty work is stressful due to the potential for nonreappointment, which is particularly onerous for adjuncts. Nonreappointment to an adjunct position can result simply from a lack of students to fill a class in a decision made at the last minute or based on negative student evaluations or other considerations. And for minoritized contingent faculty, differential expectations for performance coupled with unstable employment conditions can create a doubly high-stakes situation. As exemplified by Julie's narrative, these faculty are essentially "outsiders within" and can experience continuous pressure to prove themselves and consequently pay a high price for missteps or perceived mistakes. Little institutional support may be available whether through human resource or diversity departments or departmental or school leadership. In addition, considerable research has shown that members of nondominant groups who face marginalization and discriminatory mistreatment can experience increased vulnerability to psychosocial stresses that tax cognitive, psychological, and emotional resources, with severe health and physiological consequences.

Consider, for example, the 2017 survey conducted by the Higher Education Research Institute at the University of California, Los Angeles (UCLA) with responses from 20,771 full-time undergraduate teaching faculty members at 143 four-year colleges and universities. Stress arising from discrimination was reported by about half of Black/African American and Latino/a faculty, 30.9 percent of Asian American Pacific Islander faculty, 21.5 percent of white faculty. Interestingly, when considering the intersectionality of gender and race/ethnicity, men from minoritized groups with the exception of Asian/Pacific Islanders reported higher percentages of discrimination as a source of stress than white women.[5] Further, the "racial battle fatigue," or emotional, physiological, and psychological distress arising from everyday lived microaggressions intensifies with higher levels of educational attainment, as demonstrated in a study of 661 Black males. As a result, levels of mundane, extreme, environmental stress as documented by William A. Smith, professor and department chair at the University of Utah, and his colleagues are bound to be even more intense for minoritized faculty in predominantly white institutions in which gendered racism is present.[6]

When contingent faculty do not have other employment and health care options and are the sole breadwinner, the pressures for sheer economic survival mount. Wende Marshall, an African American disabled queer adjunct faculty member who teaches intellectual history at Temple University describes the hardships she encountered after her husband died and she went on the job market following tenure denial at the University of Virginia. Despite holding a PhD from Princeton University and a master's from Union Theological Seminary, she did not get any job offers and became virtually homeless:

> Basically the apartment that I lived in with my husband was no longer affordable after he died, and I had nowhere to go. . . . So, there were about three years where I hadn't figured out the adjunct thing and didn't have an income. I went on social security disability, and then it made it possible for me to only have one teaching gig.

The lack of a social and academic safety net for this highly qualified faculty member is a serious source of concern and underscores the potential for poverty that can follow years of academic preparation.

Consider also how Sahil, the Asian American queer male lecturer cited earlier, describes both the regularity of stress and its intensification at the end of the semester when reappointments are determined. The stress has disrupted his sleep and limited his ability to engage in healthy physical activity:

> So, I think that it's primarily, you know, mental and emotional . . . like an insecure, stressed feeling. Just feeling tense about what the future holds. And I think that those things manifest physically, so I think I hold that tension in my body. . . . Sometimes it makes it difficult to sleep, makes it difficult to, you know, just engage in healthy physical behaviors. It's pretty frequent. . . . I am reflecting on it probably on a weekly basis. I think the intensity of it varies across time, so I often feel it closer to, you know, the end of the semester when teaching assignments for the next term are being made.

For these reasons, Sahil emphasizes how difficult it is to plan a career under such uncertain circumstances when he only has four months of guaranteed employment:

> I think it's really hard to be able to plan a career when you're planning it for months at a time. So, I don't know if I'm going to have a job in January, and that's really going to be up to the university to decide, and it's like that every four months.

In essence, Sahil's elite public research university is not providing a minimal level of job security and a working environment that will allow him to thrive and attain some level of job satisfaction.

In another poignant example, Nora, the white transgender disabled faculty member introduced earlier, describes the high level of stress she experiences in an environment characterized by constant evaluation and stress. This constrained situation has amplified her feelings of depression and anxiety and taken a significant toll on her health and well-being. Her narrative highlights the terrible strain resulting both from academic pressures and inequitable performance expectations arising from intersectional minoritized status:

> In addition to being trans . . . and physically disabled, I also do suffer from depression and anxiety. And I'm certainly not blaming academia completely for this. . . . But I do think there is a lot of stress and pressure in academia, you know; whether it's your latest publication or your teaching evaluations, you're constantly being evaluated on something. And that creates a lot of stress and strain for people.
>
> And what adds to that is that when you belong to one or more marginalized groups, the pressure is greater for excellence. We've all heard the saying "Minority folks have to work twice as hard for the same results as their white counterparts or their able-bodied counterparts or their cis counterparts." And I think there is a lot of truth to that . . . and the stress and strain is terrible.

Consider also the continuous questioning of his performance experienced by Michael, an Asian American full-time contingent faculty member with administrative responsibilities in an elite midwestern public research university. Michael also describes his clear realization that he has to work harder to prove his worth, as shown in the multiple course revisions his chair assigned him during the summer months. The chair, a white female, has been reviewing his syllabi revisions in excruciating detail, a process that has not been required of other contingent faculty. As Michael explains,

> So, I feel like I'm working on three different courses at once, doing a lot of the work. And she's kind of going through things with a

fine-tooth comb, and other faculty are off. She's not checking in with them about their syllabus; they're just doing their thing. And I feel like I'm busier now compared [to] ... actually in a semester, because I'm trying to do these multiple projects and syllabi and curriculum development. I feel like it's just kind of me doing it.

Furthermore, when Michael was about to go on paternity leave, he took care to work closely with his co-instructor on making adjustments to the course they were teaching. When the leave did not allow him to fulfill the responsibilities as he had expected due to sleep deprivation, postpartum depression, and his wife's medical condition, both his supervisor and his co-instructor's supervisor notified the local human resources office that he was not fulfilling his responsibilities, and he was put on a performance plan. Michael later learned that the local office pressured his supervisor to put him on the plan and that the impetus was to have sufficient documentation should the need for nonrenewal arise. It was only with the assistance of the union and through the central human resources office that Michael was able to establish his rights through the Family Medical Leave Act. Michael describes the extreme stress arising from the situation:

And so, I had to go through the union routes; I had to go through several people ... and work with our counseling program. I went to some counseling sessions to document that I was legitimately going through some postpartum depression. So that was a very stressful time because they threatened to say "We're going to write you up. And if this happens again, you're going to have to look for another job."

The highly stressful situations and differential treatment described by Sahil, Wende Marshall, Nora, and Michael powerfully illustrate the fundamental lack of support provided by departments and institutions to minoritized contingent faculty.

INADEQUATE COMPENSATION
AND HEAVY WORKLOADS

Once individuals have served for some time in contingent faculty positions, they can become trapped in merely trying to earn a living without the time to conduct the scholarly research necessary to obtain a tenure-track position. In this regard, Nora describes the almost insurmountable difficulties of attaining a tenure-track position as similar to winning the lottery: "The goal is to get a tenure-track position. It's almost like . . . winning the lottery, to some degree, because of the corporatization of the academy into a business." Further, as Sara, an Asian American female contingent faculty member in an elite western public research university, explains,

> So, there's an oversupply of qualified PhDs who can't get tenure-track jobs. And so, it's very easy for universities to hire PhDs at very low rates because these new grads don't have anywhere to go. And a lot of those people get trapped in these sort of low-paying positions. And once they're on that circuit for a while, it's very hard to get back into a tenure-track job market search. . . . One reason is that because contingent positions are so low-paying, a lot of freshly minted PhDs are teaching at multiple universities just to barely make ends meet, so they just spend all their time teaching and driving around, and then they don't have as much time to finish their book manuscripts and peer-reviewed journal articles, all the things that you really need to be competitive.

Sara observes that due to the inadequate compensation for contingent positions, individuals who do not have other options such as an employed spouse may have to eke out a living by working at multiple institutions or even working in minimum-wage positions. The vicious circle of attempting simply to survive economically can prevent contingent faculty from conducting the research that would enhance their potential for tenure-track employment. As Sara explains,

> I try to imagine what it would be like to support just me on my salary. Forget it. I wouldn't even be able to afford rent where I live, let alone support children. I don't think it is an accident that several of my contingent faculty colleagues are unmarried, especially the men. Many of my female colleagues, the ones who have children and live comfortably, have partners who have higher salaries. The ones I know that are single really struggle to survive alone in the Bay Area. I heard of a colleague who bagged groceries at Trader Joe's to make ends meet. There was another woman who had a small child and was a single mother. She did not have enough food to feed her daughter because she had this part-time appointment and no job security or health care.

Life-changing decisions such as the decision to have a family can be affected by the lack of economic security and is especially difficult for women during their child-bearing years. Several faculty we interviewed indicated that having a spouse with a full-time tenured faculty position gave them some protection from such uncertainty. For example, Andrea, a white female adjunct who works in two or three universities simultaneously, indicates that she is only able to continue in this work due to her husband's salary and health insurance as well as her own side jobs. Moreover, if she has a gap in employment at any one of the three midwestern institutions, she has to reapply for her job, fill out the background check, and complete the I-9 and application paperwork all over again. Recently notified only a week before class started that one of her sections was underenrolled and that the course would not be run, Andrea expresses frustration about how the uncertainty of the situation is determining who can accept adjunct work, stating "I have huge concerns about that, not just on a personal level and a financial level but in regard to preparation for classes and also in regard to what it's doing to the pool of instructors that we use right now."

Due to the uncertainty of contingent roles, Andrea views adjunct faculty work as ultimately a place for rich housewives because others cannot afford to work for such minimal salaries:

> It gives me a lot of concern about who's available to do these jobs. My husband owns his own business; he's the stable income; his company picks up the health insurance. He's the one that makes this possible.... But I'm afraid that ... being an adjunct is becoming what I call the rich housewife job.... I'm afraid that what we're moving to in higher education in the contingent population is the rich housewife, the person who knows that there's a pool of money that will tide them over if something happens. And then what you're going to get is contingent faculty who say "I'm just going to do the bare minimum; design a course shell online, I'm just going to run it.... But I'm not going to put anything extra in it because you're not paying me that much."

Furthermore, when PhD recipients are unable to attain a tenure-track position after spending years in graduate school, assuming a contingent faculty position can foster a sense of inferiority and even of personal failure. Sara describes her initial feeling of inferiority as a scholar when she made the decision to pursue contingent employment in order to be located near her relatives and also have her own family. In her frank testimony she remarks, "I had to deal with a lot of like inferiority complex when all of my colleagues [in graduate school] went off to tenure-track jobs ... and for a long time, I felt like I was a failure." Yet, after having had children and a fulfilling career teaching undergraduates, Sara explains that she "made peace" with being a contingent faculty member and instead focused on the identities she cares about as a teacher, a mother, and a union activist. Through her union, Sara is working alongside her colleagues to establish a contract that secures better pay, job security, and benefits for contingent faculty.

Because of the common nature of these insecure and inadequately compensated working conditions for minoritized faculty, serious institutional attention needs to be given to ameliorating these circumstances. We will discuss proactive contingent faculty workforce strategies and programs in chapter 5.

CURRICULAR, RESEARCH, AND PEDAGOGICAL ISSUES

Contingent faculty are often limited in terms of their ability to contribute to curricular development, course selection, independent research, and pedagogical practices. All of these practices, however, are integral to the practice of academic freedom. As a result, the marriage of contingency with faculty status subverts the long-standing educational value of academic freedom, an essential condition for faculty agency and scholarly independence.

Participation in curricular development and the ability to have input into course selection clearly vary depending on the perspective of the department chair or director as well as departmental, school, and institutional practices. While research is not usually part of the contingent faculty member's portfolio, some departments do encourage and support research. Yet, with heavy teaching loads and additional responsibilities such as additional service and administrative requirements, time may be limited for scholarly pursuits.

Further, in some doctoral research institutions, clear limits are placed on the ability of contingent faculty to serve as principal investigators. For example, Diane, an Asian American female contingent faculty member at a western public research university, reports that while tenure-track faculty can hold principal investigator status and supervise undergraduates on thesis research projects, lecturers are excluded from such activities and must apply for exemptions. When Diane received external funding to go abroad to conduct interviews and do fieldwork on a project, she was informed after she submitted her proposal to the university's Institutional Review Board that she could not hold principal investigator status and could not conduct her own research. As she indicates, "But I was shocked. They were like 'you can't do anything with your data since your status is pending.' I was writing a chapter and writing my book proposal." After she talked to her chair and the chair spoke with the dean, the dean applied for an exemption on her behalf. Diane emphasizes the clear disparities in the system. "The system is not set up to treat us equally; it almost excludes you, categorically. That's really scary." Diane was subsequently granted three years to work on the research project, after which she would need to apply again to a new dean. While her persistence prevailed in this instance, the substantial hurdles posed by the process would clearly dissuade other contingent faculty from pursuing independent research.

Justin, the Black male clinical professor at an elite private university cited earlier, describes how his scholarly work was not recognized by his department. After he had completed two edited books, his work was largely overlooked and unrecognized. Citing the surprise by the university's communication department when he mentioned his books, Justin indicates that he has had to find recognition for his work outside his school. Further, his academic credentials have been questioned, such as when his former dean contacted the coordinator of a podcast in which he was featured and asked the person in charge why he was doing it. The dean, who in fact had no background in the field, said that she did not consider Justin an expert and alleged that he was not known internationally. This overt undercutting of his work by the dean at first caused Justin to question himself, as her belittling of his credentials blended with his own childhood experiences of racialized trauma. Thinking about the impact of such experiences on successful professionals of color, Justin reflected, "I think about this . . . for those who come from school systems or settings where they were underestimated." He notes that the effects of such experiences can be devastating.

Among our interviewees, we learned of a wide range of different experiences in terms of oversight by a chairperson and discretion in course selection and pedagogical methods. At one end of the spectrum were situations in which there is virtually no direct interaction with the chair or department head. This circumstance can increase uncertainty due to the lack of feedback. At the other end of the spectrum were situations that involved micro-interventions by the chair in the curriculum and even control of teaching methods. In such situations, faculty may have little or no input into course assignments. And in more ideal circumstances, contingent faculty have input into the curriculum and some latitude in selecting the courses they want to teach.

Pressures to conform to established practices and not rock the boat can, however, limit discretion in curricular practices, particularly when contingent faculty are new. Valerie, the Black female contingent faculty member cited earlier, describes the unspoken pressure she felt in the initial stages of employment:

> I find it [the pressure] comes in the initial stages, and it is unspoken in a lot of ways. It's almost like "don't involve yourself in this; don't put too much of your opinion out there; don't rock the boat. Don't try anything new." So, there's always this expectation that I'm going to wait to speak or to even engage all the time. And there's always this expectation that I won't try anything new until invited.

In terms of micro-interventions in the pedagogical process by the chair, Michael offers an example of the power dynamic involved with his white female supervisor who is most comfortable using slides and scripted approaches to teaching. He sees her insistence on this scripted approach as a result of her view that she knows the material and has been teaching for a long time. In contrast, Michael sees the emphasis on discussion and active learning techniques rather than lecture-centered approaches as critical in multicultural learning environments.[7] Yet, as Michael describes his chair's intervention, "It's kind of almost infringing on the way that I would like to teach. And so it is kind of a battle of pedagogy, I guess, in the way we're approaching things."

At the other end of the spectrum, Sahil describes his relationship with his chair as "very nonexistent." This distance has prevented his further integration in the department. In his words,

> There really isn't a relationship. So, I applied for the job when it was posted, [and] I went through an interview process. And then I was offered the position, and then there really isn't any communication. At the end of the semester, I get an email from my chair that says "Please submit your syllabus and [list] your reflections around your teaching this term." I don't think that there's any relationship building or any intentionality around integrating me in the department.

At times, disputes around the curriculum and about how diversity is portrayed can become contentious among faculty within the department, and concerns can even reverberate up through the academic hierarchy. Julie, the biracial contingent faculty member cited earlier, reports that as a biracial individual she feels that she has to educate all the time even in relation to the focus of the curriculum. In her very first semester, she faced a highly stressful situation when she became aware of materials developed by another faculty member (materials that Julie was given to teach) that she felt were deeply problematic and racist. The materials involved blackface and other racial tropes. Julie brought her concerns up in a program meeting, and this discussion led to a virtual war within the program. She ended up spending the semester in biweekly meetings with human resources. Julie further explains:

> It started a war in the program between me and my colleague and the senior faculty to the point that I was accused of causing tensions in

the program. I spent a semester in almost weekly meetings with HR. But my chair was with me. It was so stressful, and it was really like smearing me, implying that I had insulted the colleague who put together those materials, that I had made her feel bad.

But Julie insisted on her perspective and apologized to the students regarding the racist materials. The escalation of issues to human resources accentuates the vulnerability of contingent faculty when raising concerns about the curriculum or other issues. The support of Julie's chair was critical in providing her the needed support to weather the situation successfully.

The examples shared here illustrates the ways in which minoritized faculty can be sidelined, ignored, and even have their perspectives disputed. The support of the department chair is a critical component in this equation and can facilitate greater empowerment and participation.

THE DISPROPORTIONATE IMPACT OF STUDENT EVALUATIONS

Due to the lack of security that characterizes contingent faculty employment, the student is placed in the driver's seat as both consumer and faculty evaluator. One of the primary concerns that undercuts the quality of the educational experience is overreliance on student evaluations as the sole measure of the performance of a contingent faculty member. Placing control in the hands of the students can lead to pressures on contingent faculty to give higher grades in order to ensure positive evaluations. The unfortunate result can be to avoid difficult topics, placate students, inflate grades, and dilute academic quality in the interests of academic survival.[8]

A growing and substantial body of research indicates that evaluations can be skewed by bias based on the faculty member's social identities and, in particular, due to the intersectionality of race and gender. Challenges for women of color have been shown to affect perceived academic competence and legitimacy and be overly focused on physical attractiveness and demeanor.[9] Earlier we cited the 2021 meta-analysis of over one hundred articles that found that women, people of color, and other marginalized groups are disadvantaged in student evaluations.[10]

Nonetheless, Sara explains that the primary basis for promotions for contingent faculty at her institution are based on student evaluations of teaching:

> As anyone knows, teaching evaluations are skewed and ... full of racial and gender bias. But the university continues to use them. ... And so in that sense, I think that's unfair, because we know that hurts women in general. ... We know that evaluations work against us, so we have to make an extra effort to make sure that students enjoy our class. ... So, I would put myself in the category of women and minorities who, in a sense, have to try to compensate for race and gender bias in student evaluations.

Despite the known flaws in the evaluation process, Sara indicates that department chairs resort to student evaluations in order to have a specific numerical rating as an expedient way of gauging instruction:

> You know, they'd rather just have a number. This is your student evaluation number, and that's how we compare you against everyone else and decide whether you're worth promoting or not. And so, I think this system is fundamentally unfair and problematic.

The employment perils resulting from overreliance on student evaluations is intensified for marginalized faculty. Nora describes how the double jeopardy of being a member of a marginalized group and in a marginalized employment status compounds the power that students wield through evaluations:

> You feel marginalized to begin with because you're contingent faculty. You worry about being given another contract to continue on in your

position. Then you add on being a member of marginalized groups on top of that, so that adds more pressure and stress and strain[,] . . . more because of the microaggressions and the implicit bias.

. . . [T]his student wields a certain amount of power, and you want to maintain your integrity, of course, but you are worried that they could go up the chain and complain about this to your chair, to your dean, God forbid to your provost. And so, I've had students start at the level of the president, you know, with different concerns. . . . And here's the thing where you have to be concerned about grading, when you belong to these marginalized groups and when you're a contingent faculty member.

Given these circumstances, Sahil indicates that adjunct faculty can be reluctant to give lower grades because of how this might reflect on their teaching:

I have many friends who are tenure-track faculty members, and I think that they spend a lot of time making sure that there's a distribution within their grades. . . . It's very important to them to have a distribution. And I think that when I look at my grades, I'm afraid to have a distribution, because if I have three or four people who have C's in my class, like, one, they're not going to give me a great evaluation, but two, it also tells the department that I am not a good educator when there are all the[se] students who are getting bad grades.

A number of our interviewees also indicated that students can knowingly seek to affect a contingent faculty member's status through evaluations. Based on his prior experience as an academic adviser, Sahil believes that students are aware of the power they exert over contingent faculty appointments and they use that power strategically:

I often heard students talk about like if a faculty member told them that they couldn't have an excused absence, how that's something that they were going to make sure to put in the final teaching evaluation[,] ... so I do think that students are strategic about that.

Similarly, LeeAnn describes her awareness as an administrator of how students have banded together to give negative evaluations to certain nontenured faculty members such as those who are not native English speakers:

> On several occasions as an administrator at different institutions, particularly for nontenured faculty members, [I observed] that students decided, for example, because of an accent or because that person was speaking English as a second language, a group of students didn't think that they should be teaching economics or an introductory course in psychology. I've seen students band together and deliberately give some very harsh remarks about faculty members.... Students can use the evaluation process in a very manipulative way.

Several of the contingent faculty members we spoke with also described lengthy grade appeal processes that involved protracted negotiations over student complaints and created great stress for them. Take the case of Monica, cited earlier, one of the only Black female contingent faculty members in a predominantly white midwestern public research university. During the summer of her first year as a lecturer after she had filed her grades and left campus, a white male student who received a B instead of an A filed a formal complaint of discrimination based on race and contested the grade all the way up to the provost. Monica describes how her hypervisibility as a Black woman contributed to the questioning of her academic credentials:

> But I am the only Black woman lecturer, and ... I know when I go to lecture gatherings and union gatherings, I stick out like a sore thumb. And then I stick out amongst my tenure-track colleagues, so I know

that that difference is clear and is seen. . . . I think that probably speaks [to] probably some of the most racist and classist things that happened to me . . . because it's there, it's embedded. I'm not even necessarily shown it. . . . It's more of a surprise or curiosity or a fascination like "you really teach here" or "you really have that job?"

The complaint by the student was, in her words, "fraught with everything having to do with racism and sexism in classes." While Monica's faculty colleagues were supportive of her and reassured her that nothing like that had ever happened before, she realized they did not understand the extent to which the situation derived from her minoritized identity. As she observes, "I think it would have been different if I were a man. . . . Obviously it was about race, and so the intersection of race and gender." Furthermore, Monica believes that the mistreatment she experienced was a function of her Blackness combined with her gender, class, and age:

I think that if I was another race or ethnicity or were just nonwhite, I think that would not bother them, but I do particularly think there was something about my Blackness to bother them. And I think even in the ways that they questioned my degree. . . . I also think that has to do with perceived class, and how they think about my age and my status like. . . . I couldn't possibly, I couldn't possibly, have earned the degree that I clearly have earned.

For Monica, as a new lecturer, the complaint and its ramifications triggered a sense of not belonging, or the impostor syndrome. She was keenly aware of her status and the potential for the complaint to dislodge her from academia:

Part of what made that experience so terrifying for me was that my impostor syndrome was triggered that much more because even though I intellectually knew I hadn't done anything wrong, I felt like this is the moment they're going to figure out that I shouldn't be here. Like ... this is going to be where they figure out she doesn't belong here anyway, and we can just let her go.

Monica was terrified, since she had not yet had a chance to establish herself at the university and did not know any of the higher-level administrators:

And because I'm a lecturer, I think I was also terrified. ... I was a very new contingent faculty; no one knows me. I hadn't had time to let anyone get to know my skills or what kind of educator I am, and the first thing that I am ever in contact with higher-level administrators is around something like this.

The parents of the student soon became involved, and as Monica explains, they "were really angry." They openly questioned Monica's qualifications, refusing to believe that she held a doctorate and claiming that she had lied about her degree:

They wrote lots of emails and lots of notes. ... They didn't believe that I had a PhD. They claimed that I had lied and didn't have a PhD, and so they wanted to be assured that I actually had earned my degree. ... It became this different thing. They couldn't possibly be okay with the fact that somebody like me was teaching and that I had given their child a grade that they thought wasn't good enough.

The mother of the student even wrote a note disclaiming the fact that their family was racist, stating, "I think you all think that we're racist but we have black people in our family so we couldn't possibly be racist." In response to the reverse discrimination complaint, Monica had to produce her records and explain her grading process to the higher-level administrators, whom she found to be generally supportive. Given the highly stressful ordeal, she was tempted to change the grade just to make the situation end but ultimately decided against it. After the case was finally closed, the provost wrote a memo to file indicating that her work was sound and stating that her contributions were valuable. Yet, the egregious nature of the discrimination claim and the protracted stress, anxiety, and even terror Monica experienced underscore the extreme vulnerability faced by minoritized contingent faculty in their efforts to uphold academic standards.

In another example, David, the contingent Latino faculty member cited earlier, describes how one his students filed a formal grade complaint regarding an A– when the student believed it should have been an A. The complaint went all the way up to the program director and department chair and became a part of his official record. The chair, who was also Latino, was supportive of David but tried to give him advice along the lines of "don't rock the boat" and "don't push it so hard." But David found this advice hard to accept at the time, since he knew that the student was not justified. As David explains, "So, I didn't like the idea that I had to, in some way, change my teaching style because of something I thought was unfair, unjust."

David also indicates that he has received teaching evaluations criticizing him for being too open. "I've had those evaluations for being too proud, for being too open, for not giving the racists and misogynists enough empathy and perspective." He is sanguine, however, about such evaluations. "At this point I shrug my shoulders, and as a nontenured faculty, you kind of just have to accept this in order not to die of stress and anxiety that you might not have a job every year." He adds,

> With regard to teaching critical race theory or talking about things where there's going to be an immediate bias, I kind of just don't care, because I figure you are going to dislike me, regardless, even if I said the thing that you wanted. I've seen that happen many times. . . . So, I take it as par for the course; that's going to be the reality.

Valerie, the Black contingent faculty referenced earlier, describes the racism she has encountered in the evaluation process and how white male students have challenged whether she is qualified to teach them:

> It's usually responses where the students themselves are challenging me, challenging whether I know what I'm talking about or not. Usually male students, usually white students, who will challenge and suddenly say "she didn't do this/she didn't say that," and they always challenge the fact that I am qualified to teach them. And I've had very specific racial experiences around that kind of feedback.

In one instance when a student claimed in an evaluation that Valerie had bullied him and showed favoritism to other students, an unofficial investigation was undertaken without her knowledge. She only learned of it from overhearing other students who had been individually interviewed talking about it. "The situation was investigated behind my back," she said, "and I wasn't told that I was being investigated, so they interviewed other students, [and] I just happened to overhear students talking about being separated and interviewed around the student." The student later denied that he had made the allegation and said he couldn't remember writing it. The handling of this incident represented a violation of standard human resource investigative practices in which individuals are notified of allegations and have a right to respond.

Further, Justin, the Black male clinical faculty member cited earlier, was explicitly told when he was hired that if he failed a student, the student would complain to the dean, and Justin would be asked to go back and change the grade. He was cautioned to "be very careful of the grades you leave, because [they] could look bad on your evaluation now even though you judge the student accordingly." As a result, Justin notes that the department has allowed students to get by until recently, when a shift occurred as the school was trying to raise its ratings. As Justin explains, "now they want to talk about quality. Before it was about money and especially if they [the students] had VA [Veterans' Administration] money."

All these examples illustrate the significant pressures resulting from student complaints and negative evaluations that can undermine and even threaten the employment status of contingent faculty. The continuous stress arising from employment-related threats can take a significant toll on the faculty member's health and well-being, with long-term consequences.

LACK OF PARTICIPATION IN SHARED GOVERNANCE

The structural inequity of the two-tiered faculty model is particularly apparent in faculty governance proceedings when part- and full-time contingent faculty cannot participate and are not represented. In some institutions, contingent faculty and especially adjuncts do not hold the right to vote in department meetings, college proceedings, and faculty senates or councils. This exclusion affects their ability to participate in academic decision-making such as in curricular planning and development, chair selection, and recruitment and hiring.

Clearly, some progress has been made in the inclusion of full-time contingent faculty members in academic governance processes. The 2021 American Association of University Professors shared governance survey found that in a random sample of 585 four-year institutions with an academic senate or council, at 75.6 percent of the institutions full-time contingent faculty members can vote in elections, and at 69.7 percent of the institutions they can serve on the senate or council itself. Only 6.9 percent of institutions preclude all full-time contingent faculty from voting, and 11.3 percent do not allow these faculty to serve on the senate. These figures represent improvement from 2001, when at 17 percent of institutions only full-time tenure-line faculty could vote.[11]

The same progress, however, has not been achieved for part-time contingent faculty or adjuncts. The survey revealed that at 66.5 percent of institutions, part-time faculty members cannot vote, while at 72.2 percent they cannot serve on senates or councils.[12] A 2012 American Association of University Professors report titled "The Inclusion in Governance of Faculty Members Holding Contingent Appointments" emphasized that faculty governance and academic freedom reinforce each other and recommended that faculty should be defined inclusively and not limited to those holding tenured or tenure-track appointments. For this reason, the report recommended that all part-time and full-time contingent faculty play a role in academic governance. The report stated that contingent faculty should have responsibilities in governance similar to their tenure-line counterparts and should receive compensation for their time participating in governance activities.[13]

Although greater participation of part-time faculty typically occurs at the departmental level, when these faculty who now represent the faculty majority cannot participate in college or institutional governance, they do not have the opportunity to share perspectives and provide input into policies and practices. Further, James Minor persuasively argues that administrative efforts to diversity faculty have largely been unsuccessful and that faculty diversity will benefit from the ability to include women and minorities in academic governance and decision-making processes.[14] Greater interactions of tenure-line faculty with contingent faculty and particularly minoritized contingent faculty is an important vehicle for reducing tensions and breaking down negative stereotypes and images such as the idea that non-tenure-track faculty are not quality scholars and are in some way "less than."[15]

At her eastern public research university, Julie describes how contingent faculty are encouraged to attend college faculty meetings "just to show the numbers." But since the meetings describe privileges she does not hold as a lecturer, she explains, "I don't always go to those meetings because it's very depressing." Julie also notes that her lecturer colleagues do not often speak up during the meetings and that when she speaks up she has noticed that tenure-track faculty interrupt her constantly.

Similarly, Nora indicates that the full-time tenure-line faculty recently voted to exclude contingent faculty from voting in her college. As she explains, "Although it was a close vote, lecturers understandably were very upset about this happening." In this regard, she notes, "I feel more accepted overall by contingent faculty than I do by tenure-track faculty."

Faculty governance can provide a significant avenue for breaking down the barriers among faculty cohorts through the creation of unified initiatives that influence institutional decision-making and provide a needed voice for the concerns of contingent faculty.

CONCLUSION

Through the narratives shared in this chapter, we have seen how uncertain employment conditions, low pay levels, fluctuating health insurance coverage, lack of control over work circumstances, heavy workloads, differential treatment, and excessive reliance on student evaluations work in combination to reinforce the marginalization faced by minoritized contingent faculty. While some students may be unaware of the status-based differences that pertain to these faculty, the devaluation of teaching represented in the two-tiered faculty employment model jeopardizes academic quality, student learning outcomes, and sustainability.

Just as importantly, the perpetuation of an inequitable structure undermines the faculty talent proposition and leads to a tremendous waste of talent. The impressive credentials of the contingent faculty we interviewed powerfully illustrate the limited opportunities available in a saturated academic job market. While all the interviewees care immensely about their disciplines and their students, their commitment cannot be taken for granted. As Andrea, the white female adjunct cited earlier, states, "I think we're sitting on a decision point, I think we have been for several years, and it was accelerated by COVID." She emphasizes that without attention to the employment conditions of contingent faculty, higher education will lose individuals with institutional loyalty who are invested in the educational process. The examples shared in this chapter provide significant evidence of the pressing need for institutional change and the development of inclusive policies, processes, and programs for contingent faculty.

In chapter 4, we explore specific strategies that minoritized contingent faculty have developed to resist and cope with inequitable employment conditions.

4

Resilient Coping Strategies of Minoritized Contingent Faculty

You must come to grips with the fact that you are
fighting for a cause bigger than yourself.
WILLIAM A. SMITH, IN *RACIAL BATTLE*
FATIGUE IN FACULTY

G iven the everyday workplace challenges faced by contingent faculty from nondominant groups, we now share concrete strategies and proactive approaches that can help counteract structural, behavioral, and process-based barriers to inclusion. While individual approaches are certainly important, long-term structural change is critical in order to create more equitable working conditions. An important first step is the creation of a representative bureaucracy that includes diverse academic administrators. With an increasingly diverse student body, the continued dominance of white male heterosexist perspectives is not responsive to changing student needs.[1] As Michael, the Asian American contingent faculty member cited earlier, observes,

I believe we still operate in a system of oppression, where white people are in positions of power. And until we get minority faculty in positions of authority in directors and dean's roles ... where they understand from firsthand experience what it means to be a person of color, I don't think we're going to see a lot of change. And I think to get into those positions is a very uphill battle.

Yet, in situations of unequal power, only significant countervailing forces can provide some measure of protection against marginalization, mistreatment, and discrimination. In this regard, the perpetrator-guardian model developed by Vincent Roscigno, Steven Lopez, and Randy Hodson in 2009, based on 204 book-length organizational ethnographies, recognizes that women, minorities, and individuals with little job security are more at risk for bullying and mistreatment in ambiguous organizational situations. As these ethnographies demonstrate, the presence of a capable guardian can help offset and neutralize such situations. Unions have served in the guardian role due to the sheer power of numbers and the benefit derived from collective efforts to create working environments that are less tolerant of capricious management practices and that provide redress through mediation and grievance procedures.[2] Since adjuncts and full-time contingent faculty have few if any employment protections, it is not surprising that the most frequently mentioned countervailing force cited by our interviewees is unionization.

UNIONIZATION: A GROWING TREND

Because colleges and universities have relegated contingent faculty concerns to the periphery of the educational enterprise, unions have stepped in to address working conditions and negotiate for limited but needed improvements. Researchers Kim Tolley and Kristen Edwards view the organizing of adjuncts as one of the most important trends affecting higher education. Their in-depth analysis of collective bargaining contracts ratified between 2010 and 2016 at thirty-five colleges and universities reveals that adjunct faculty obtained salary increases at all these institutions through negotiation processes. Further, almost all the contracts increased job security for contingent faculty such as through full-year and even multiyear appointments for adjuncts. Other gains have included access to professional development and improved resources for teaching. Nonetheless, in terms of needed structural changes, unionization has not made inroads in three critical areas: achieving parity in salary and benefits with tenure-line faculty, participation in shared governance, and decreasing the reliance on part-time faculty.[3]

Although unions cannot reverse the large-scale stratification of the academic workforce, one of the primary benefits of unionization is having a seat at the table with university administration. In the absence of active management attention to contingent faculty concerns, union activism has become the most effective driver of change. Such activism is most effective when tenured faculty join forces with contingent faculty in a collaborative effort. Because tenure-line faculty unions have substantially more clout in the negotiation process, the coalition of tenured and contingent faculty provides a significantly stronger bargaining position. Many universities with tenure-line faculty unions wait for the results of negotiations before providing similar increases or benefits changes for management and staff. As a result, the solidarity between tenured and adjunct faculty unions can serve as a critical lever that increases the likelihood of successful negotiated outcomes.

Different models for unionization include the inclusion of contingent and tenure-line faculty within the same union umbrella or separate representation by separate bargaining agents. Regardless of the mode of representation, the alliance of interests between tenure-line and contingent faculty can create significant pressure on the administration for change.

While unions as a whole have little ability to counteract nonrenewal of adjuncts due to the limitations of term-based contracts, they have been able to provide limited assistance such as in negotiations of earlier notification deadlines and dispute resolution. The narratives of our interviewees reveal that unions also have served as a buffer or protective force in mediating complex employee relations disputes. Several contingent faculty we spoke with emphasized how their unions had helped them in difficult situations by representing their interests, participating in meetings with management, and providing some measure of protection.

Others mentioned their own activism in union work including efforts to include adjuncts in the union.

Take the work of Tanya, a white female contingent faculty union president in an eastern public research university, who describes the union's efforts to make the system safer through contract negotiations, push up notification of nonrenewal before September of each year, and establish different ways to measure faculty performance other than total reliance on student evaluations. She refers to the work situation as the "Wild West" before the union arrived, with "wildly different teaching arrangements" and individuals with PhDs paid as low as $28,000 with full teaching loads. In another example, Wende Marshall, the African American disabled queer contingent faculty member mentioned earlier, indicates that she sees her union activism at Temple University and in community organizing as the primary reasons for remaining at the university:

> I've been very involved with community organizing around Temple, which is a poor historically Black community facing an onslaught of gentrification. And so, I also have the perspective of the way the university treats the community. I'm in this job because I want to be a union activist, not because I like teaching. What I teach is not what I was trained to teach.

It must also be noted, however, that even union leadership may not reflect the racial diversity of their membership. Nicholas Hartlep, a Korean transracial adoptee who now serves as department chair in the School of Urban Education at Metropolitan State University, describes what he calls "the white space" of the union. Despite his pro-union stance, he recounts how the all-white union leadership publicly recalled him as a unit convener in a humiliating fashion for requesting that a faculty member revise her dossier for tenure and promotion. In an act of further retaliation, the union attempted to hold a recall vote to remove him from his position as department chair, resulting in a consultant being hired by the dean and the provost to interview faculty about the climate in the School of Urban Education. As a result, Hartlep concludes that faculty unions can play an inadvertent role in preserving white supremacy.[4]

PROACTIVE CAREER PLANNING

As a preemptive strategy, several full-time non-tenure-track faculty we interviewed described the steps they are taking to obtain greater job security by moving to the next rung of the contingent career ladder. This progression is generally accompanied by longer contract lengths of up to five years and increased salary increments, bringing with it less likelihood of being laid off. For example, at the University of California, lecturers can be appointed as faculty "with potential for security of employment" and progress in the hierarchy to obtain what are termed continuing appointments, or those with "security of employment."[5] This hybrid professorial model gives substantial stability and creates a closer parallel with the tenure-line model. Notably, however, the compensation structures remain below the tenure-track model. At one University of California campus, for example, lecturers with potential for security are subject to an excellence review after ten semesters and with successful completion of the review become eligible for continuing appointment after the completion of twelve semesters. Attainment of the continuing appointment means that the faculty member does not receive an annual letter of appointment and, in effect, is much less likely to be discontinued. However, the availability of continuing appointments can vary considerably by campus and by department. One adjunct faculty member employed for nearly five decades at a University of California campus indicated that obtaining such appointments was extremely rare in her department.

David, the Latino faculty member at a southwestern public research university cited earlier, describes his efforts to move up the lecturer ladder to the next rank in order to protect himself from possible future layoff.

He explains his strategy: "It certainly motivated me to take on as many opportunities as I could. Sometimes more than I wanted to because I wanted to be sure my CV looked impressive; my promotion packet looked pretty stacked." David notes that attainment of the promotion does give him somewhat more security but indicates that he would still like to move up even further, since the university is not hiring many more instructional faculty. He also believes that because his wife is a tenured professor who brings in a great deal of research money to the university, he has a little more security.

While a viable protective strategy, such career planning alternatives may be more difficult to attain for more senior members of the workforce, particularly for women and individuals of color.[6] Research indicates that the intersectionality of more advanced age with other minoritized identities can preclude consideration based on the perception that future contributions will be limited.[7] In some cases, ageism can trump all other stereotypes and dominate all other stereotypical perceptions Women in particular can experience the penalties of ageism as early as their forties based on social expectations related to appearance.[8] As a result, ageism can limit opportunities significantly and make alternative career pathways less feasible.

COUNTERACTING DIFFERENTIAL STANDARDS AND STRESS

As described throughout the book, differential expectations in relation to performance for minoritized faculty are a powerful marker of inequality. But often these expectations can be couched in ambiguous statements or masked through disingenuous behavior. Although often difficult to pinpoint or discern, the method of transmission of such expectations can be through the questioning of competence, excessive scrutiny and criticism, subtle comments, and failure to support individuals by providing mentoring and feedback. More consequential acts of exclusionary treatment can be preceded by the creation of unequal working conditions such as the assignment of tasks that others may not be asked to perform.[9] For individuals encountering differential treatment, confusion can arise as to which components (e.g., race, gender, sexual orientation, disability, age) are the source of exclusionary behaviors.[10] And when signals and behaviors are ambiguous, stigmatized individuals can overlook and fail to decode them.

The psychological literature offers insight into such situations through the concept of attributional ambiguity in which individuals find it difficult to interpret ambiguous behaviors, whether positive or negative, and are unsure of whether to attribute the behaviors to prejudice.[11] Contraindications such as smiles and overly effusive behavior can disguise biased and even threatening motives and cause confusion.[12] When such signals by institutional gatekeepers lead to consequential forms of exclusion, the danger lies in not pursuing timely countermeasures. A critical first step is cognitive appraisal of a situation and evaluation of the potential for threat, challenge, or harm (primary appraisal).[13] The process of secondary appraisal gauges the availability of coping options and resources.

An important insight from research findings is that appropriately attributing negative actions to prejudice can provide a self-protective function to individuals who are the targets of discriminatory behavior and can help diminish emotional reactions to these behaviors. In such cases, a stigmatized individual's self-esteem is not affected negatively when the individual can appropriately attribute negative behaviors or outcomes to perceived racism.[14]

Consistent with these research findings, Monica, the Black contingent faculty member cited earlier, manages to maintain a rather constant level of low-grade stress by recognition of the structural nature of oppression. This recognition essentially provides an everyday protective mechanism by depersonalizing the nature of exclusionary treatment. Further, she takes comfort from interacting with colleagues with whom she can discuss openly the impact of their social identities on work experiences. At the same time, however, Monica finds it more difficult to maintain this approach when interacting with colleagues in other departments who may not find value in her department's work. She describes the racism, classism, and sexism she finds as being deeply rooted in the organizational culture of her prestigious university:

> I know that working at a prestigious American university, racism, classism, and sexism are just baked in. . . . Because they're so structural, I don't even know that these things are happening. And so that's like a low-grade type of stress that I just manage everyday . . . around race and white supremacy and class. . . . I think it varies; most days it's manageable. I think I find it being less manageable and more stressful maybe certain times of the year. But I feel very able to manage or navigate a lot of those things with my colleagues because that's the kind of work we do and we can have more open conversations about how our identities impact our work life and what we're doing. I think it gets more stressful when I'm interacting with departments, people who don't necessarily find value in our work—when I feel I have to prove something about myself or about my work.

The strategy Monica identifies of finding a trusted internal network of allies with whom one can openly discuss issues of identity can provide some solidarity and support in addressing exclusionary workplace situations.

Taking another tack, Valerie, the Black contingent faculty member referenced earlier, has developed a counterstrategy when experiencing pressures to work harder in order to prove her worth. For example, she was questioned by another faculty member as to whether she was experiencing impostor syndrome, with the underlying insinuation that she was barely getting by as an affirmative action candidate. Valerie catches herself when she responds to such pressures by overcompensating and instead tries to find ways to work smarter rather than harder:

But as a result of that I do find that there are times that I slip and I find myself working too hard to kind of overcompensate for those moments. Recently I've been catching myself on that, and I don't work too hard; I have to work smarter.

Valerie's resistance strategy involves recognition of the triggers or situations that can cause her to overcompensate by working harder, and she instead responds proactively by devising more calculated approaches to the problems at hand.

SEEKING EXTERNAL
ALTERNATIVES AND SUPPORT

When problematic situations escalate and particularly when they involve issues of mistreatment and marginalization, serious consideration has to be given as to whether to seek confidential assistance from human resources, an ombudsperson, the employee assistance program, or the office that handles diversity, equity, and inclusion. In making this choice, individuals must weigh the potential for making their claims known and the value of establishing an institutional record of issues against concerns relating to the potential breach of confidentiality that can result.

In this regard, Nadine, an Asian American contingent faculty member, recounts a difficult situation during her first year of employment in which an older white male colleague shared a workspace with her and essentially engaged in workplace harassment toward her. The male faculty member would leave his sandals and socks under his desk and his belongings strewn about the office. She would often come into the office and find his students sitting at her desk. Once when this occurred and the student tried to get up from her desk out of courtesy to her, the male faculty member instead told the student to stay there while they finished their conversation. When Nadine reported the incident to administration, the male faculty member sent her a nasty email attacking her and saying she was passive aggressive and did not know how to share.

As she explains, "I was worried about my job. It was only the first year that I was teaching there, and I thought 'I just want to put it behind me.' I'm just going to walk away from it." Yet, Nadine describes the intensification of the situation:

> But it got very heated the way we shared this space, and he was just a very dominant person, and I was kind of intimidated by this guy. And did he treat me that way because I was a woman? Yes, definitely[;] . . . he thought himself more senior [than] me when in reality he really wasn't, and he just felt that the place was his.

Nonetheless, when Nadine brought the situation up with her administrator, she was told not to tell the dean or anybody else and that the administrator would handle it. To her consternation, she was then moved into an office with two other people, while the male faculty member was given an office to himself. "Looking back again," Nadine said, "I should have filed a complaint with the university, but I didn't. I trusted she would handle it." Now as a seasoned faculty member, Nadine views the situation differently:

> Years later I thought to myself, hmm, that doesn't seem right. I was with this abusive guy. And they just validated his behavior by allowing him to have the whole office to himself, while they just get rid of the one who's complaining.

ORGANIZATIONAL SPONSORSHIP

Finding a support system such as with a sponsor or mentor within the institution is a valuable strategy that can help overcome internal obstacles and offset negative feedback. Sponsorship is distinct from mentorship in that individuals who have significant power and organizational clout can advocate for their protégés and protect them from potentially negative consequences by intervening at higher levels of the organization. Yet, a study of forty high-potential individuals found that such sponsorship is less available for women, with the result that women overworked their mentorship channels even though their mentors had less organizational clout.[15] As the study reveals, minoritized faculty may find it more difficult to locate a sponsor who is willing to step in and help them overcome institutional obstacles. Lack of diversity in academic and administrative leadership can make it more challenging to find individuals to sponsor women and women of color and assist in their progress.

Consider the valuable example of sponsorship that LeeAnn, the African American administrator and contingent faculty member, received from her white female Jewish program director. The program director first hired her for the small department and then voluntarily took on the role of full-time faculty coach. As an adjunct faculty member without even an office, LeeAnn faced challenges in connecting with classes of nontraditional students who were working full time and also often parenting. In addition, as an African American female, she states, "My credibility was tested and challenged on the part of the students, and there wasn't a collective place of support that I could go to and say 'Hey, is this happening for you in your classroom?'"

LeeAnn describes the program director as assisting her both emotionally and mentally, whereas the institution's support was "certainly lacking." She felt particularly fortunate, since her program director was trained in relational cultural counseling and had a PhD in counseling. LeeAnn indicated that due to the program director's religious background and the history of persecution faced by the Jews, "it was easy to talk to her about the ways in which I felt that some students attacked me or questioned my credibility." LeeAnn credits this ease of communication to her coach having been in similar situations and been discriminated against, "and so it made our conversations much easier [because] I didn't have to prove or explain."

In her role as faculty coach, the program director helped LeeAnn by addressing both the technical aspects of teaching and the reactions she received from students. This support reinforced LeeAnn's confidence in her own competence and teaching ability:

> Intellectually, I felt that I had the makings of a good teacher, based on my education, based on my experiences [and] . . . on the research that I've done. But I don't think it takes much for that kind of confidence to be attacked, or penetrated, if the student experience isn't one where you're getting that enthusiasm on a regular basis. . . . She helped me through not beating myself up after every lecture.

Further, the coaching and mentorship that LeeAnn received from her program director helped her navigate the complexities of teaching in the institution more rapidly:

> And so, having this kind of coach allowed me to read and understand the university a lot quicker, because this individual had some longevity at the university, and they were able to help me maneuver and get through some of these challenges.

The encouragement that LeeAnn received from her program director included support in completing her PhD. Overall, LeeAnn describes the chair's sponsorship with some modesty: "She sees a brilliance in me (she uses this word, I don't) that I don't see in myself." LeeAnn adds that "it's all about having a chair that wants to be a coach, wants to be a mentor, wants to see you succeed."

BEING AUTHENTIC:
AGENCY AND SELF-DETERMINATION

As the minoritized faculty we interviewed have faced marginalization and exclusion, they have also exhibited remarkable courage in affirming their own identities and modeling this authenticity for their students.

Despite their isolation in predominantly white institutions with few diverse faculty colleagues, several individuals spoke of the difficult decision to openly discuss their identities in their largely white classrooms despite the emotional costs. In this regard, Becky Ropers-Huilman, professor at the University of Minnesota, points out that people whose "cultural homes" are not well represented in dominant society may feel that they need to mask themselves based on their degree of fit within the society at large. Like the construction of a dance, masking and unmasking occurs based on an individual's reading of the social context.[16]

In describing his decision to unmask, Sahil indicates that once he discusses his identity in his classes, particularly as a queer person from a low-income family, students begin to challenge him more and also challenge his grading policies more:

> I mean, I spend a lot of time talking about my identity and about what it's like to be a person who lives in those identities. And I think one of the things that I've noticed is . . . when I share that I come from an immigrant family or that I am queer, I think that it changes the way in which my students interact with me. . . . At the beginning of the semester before I made those disclosures, I think I command respect because of probably my gender, because I'm an Asian American man, and I think there were some expectations that Asian American men are intelligent and belong in academia. But I think once my students get to know me . . . they start to challenge me a little bit more; they start to challenge course policies a little bit more; they start to challenge my grading a little bit more.

Similarly, David feels it important to discuss his identity as a first-generation minoritized scholar in his predominantly white classrooms. David's parents emigrated from Cuba and were working-class individuals. His father was an electrician, and a significant portion of David's life was spent living on food stamps and welfare. He had to think hard about sharing his identity in the large undergraduate sections he taught. But despite the rather rural geographic location of his predominantly white university, David decided to discuss his race and ethnicity because he felt that his openness would benefit his students:

> I decided to go in there and be loud and proud. I guess the idea is . . . if you're going to dislike me, I'm going to give you a damn good reason to dislike me. I'm not going to hide myself and then hope that you like this watered-down version of myself. I really hit it hard because I wanted that not to be hidden, and I was trying to think about things I would have wanted when I was a young scholar. I didn't remember anyone saying outwardly like "this is my race or ethnicity" apart from very specific kinds of classes.

Nonetheless, David indicates that disclosing his identity so openly to his students required significant emotional labor. Fortunately, however, he reports that he only really experienced one negative interaction in response.

Consonant with this perspective, Nora, the transgender disabled faculty member cited earlier, is aware that she is not the typical professor that students expect to have but nonetheless seeks to be authentic in representing herself:

> There's always this push and pull between the way I see myself and the way that others see me, and that includes the way the students see me. When I walk in the door on the first day of class, what are they thinking? You know, I'm not the typical professor that they may be envisioning. And I have to keep that in mind and play it to some degree and use it as an advantage, so that if I'm the first transgender person they've met that I will make a good impression. But more importantly, it is just being authentic[,] . . . being who you really are and trying to

model that for them so they can also be that as well, because there's so much pressure on them to conform.

In another example, Monica indicates that she is aware that she is one of the few Black women her students have had as a professor in a predominantly white institution. At the same time, she finds that students of color from working-class backgrounds like her own see themselves in her and are encouraged by her example. For the most part, however, students do not understand that she is a lecturer even when she explains the difference between tenure-track and non-tenure-track positions:

> I've been aware since I started here that many students—whether they share social identities that I have or not—I'm one of the few Black women that they've ever had as a college professor. . . . But most are surprised to see someone like me as a college professor, and many welcome it. . . . I have a few students who talked about wanting to become academics; they want to go on to graduate school. And I don't think it is an accident that a lot of those students who say that to me are also young women of color from low-income backgrounds who grew up working class like I did. . . .
>
> So, I think in some ways they see a bit of themselves or a least a bit of their background in me, and that encourages them or lets them know that it is possible to do this kind of work. And most of them don't know that I'm a lecturer. And so, when I explain to them what that means, they are like "aren't you still a professor?" And I say "yes," but I explain to them the difference between tenure-track jobs and non-tenure-track jobs, and I still think they don't quite get it.

In the face of marginalization and even mistreatment, Monica describes the evolution of her own sense of agency in spite of the negative attributes accorded to her due to her race and gender. She emphasizes her pride in her lineage and how the negative experiences she has had in a predominantly white institution have helped her define who she is:

> I know for Black people outside of those groups, I know that those identities come with tons of stereotypes, tons of negative attitudes, and I think even given that there's so much for me about having those identities, . . . I think is very important to me, very special to me. You know, some of those attributes . . . connect me to a really important lineage that I'm proud to be a part of.
>
> I actually think, you know, the experiences that I've had here even as horrible or as trying as some of them have been, . . . I think they've helped me define who I am and figure out who I am, in context, and so . . . I think I've gained more of a sense of being able to define myself as opposed to sort of losing that. . . . I know that people outside of me, . . . you know, folks with various identities, have a lot more power and collectively have the power to cast projections on me—[of that] I'm completely aware—*but I think that I still retain some real agency.* But, I think that one of the things coming from particular marginalized backgrounds [is that] I've inherited the ability to be able to define myself and understand who I am.

Monica clearly has drawn on the marginalizing and discriminatory experiences she has faced to develop and affirm a clear sense of identity and strengthen her internal coping and resistance resources.

CONCLUSION

In this chapter, we have seen a wide range of coping and resistance strategies deployed by minoritized contingent faculty in dealing with exclusionary behaviors, actions, and outcomes. As noted, the double jeopardy of being both a contingent faculty member and a minoritized individual can provide significant mental and physical stress on a daily basis. The resilience, courage, know-how, and persistence of the faculty members we interviewed have enabled them to address the challenges they face regularly. Perhaps most significantly, unions have been the primary catalyst for change in ensuring more equitable work circumstances, but a long road still must be traveled to narrow the gap in working conditions between tenure-line and contingent faculty.

On an individual basis, knowledge of the nature of discrimination and its manifestations has provided some benefit to minoritized contingent faculty in protecting self-esteem and developing viable counteractive strategies. And as we have seen, the advocacy of an influential sponsor or mentor can help overcome obstacles, build confidence, and solidify standing in the institution. For some individuals, proactive career planning has provided a layer of protection from layoffs or nonrenewals in uncertain financial situations.

In chapter 5, we address the current polarized environment for diversity in the United States and its impact on the experiences of minoritized contingent faculty. In light of the disruption caused by the pandemic, we look toward the future and the potential for changing educational practices and the creation of more equitable work conditions for contingent faculty.

5

Navigating Systemic Change in Contentious Times

*If the policies that created the deplorable treatment
of adjuncts persists, minority instructors like
me will continue to leave academia.*

GILA BERRYMAN, "THE SECRET LIVES
OF ADJUNCT PROFESSORS"

As we have noted, leading scholars have proposed strategies for contingent faculty employment designed to foster a more welcoming culture, develop a more equitable contingent faculty framework, and implement policies that include onboarding, professional development, and the creation of multiyear contracts with career ladders. This work, however, is still in its early and formative stages at many institutions. Furthermore, institutional diversity planning and the research literature have barely touched on the experiences of minoritized faculty in these contingent roles.

Viewed as a whole, the primary challenge for institutions in the two-tiered faculty equation is structural; that is, beginning to narrow the distance between the tenured and contingent faculty ranks within the institutional hierarchy itself. Recall how Sahil described the caste system of two-tiered faculty and the ways in which the language of lecturers versus professors reifies this distinction. Ultimately, as researcher Mark Purcell notes, the failure to critically address the institutional status of contingent faculty will undermine the intellectual and educational foundations of academe.[1] For example, one study of a non-tenure-track (NTT) school (called "PPS") within a tenure-track elite university (called "Galaxy University") highlights how power and politics significantly constrained the efforts of contingent faculty to gain institutional support in launching a faculty diversity, equity, and inclusion (DEI) initiative. Surprisingly, despite the university's significant financial resources, these contingent faculty had enormous difficulty accessing institutional resources for DEI professional development in their school. As contingent faculty, they were viewed essentially as outsiders within academe. Sarah, an Asian American female part-time faculty member, explained:[2]

> My understanding is that non-tenure-track faculty or part-time faculty like me are perceived by the institution as not credible. . . . What did spark my feeling of injustice was the lack of resources related to DEI development, as if it isn't a critical factor for our pedagogical development. The faculty status should not matter. We actually teach the majority of the student population if you account for how many there are of us versus the tenured faculty.

Maya, an African American female part-time faculty member who worked proactively with colleagues to offer the first DEI workshops in the NTT school of this elite university, also commented on the lack of equitable access to resources:[3]

> As a woman of color, it has always mattered to me to fight for access, and in many ways, the faculty of our non-tenure-track school [PPS] is viewed less than the faculty from tenure track schools at Galaxy. Professionally and personally, that is upsetting to me, as access to DEI resources, whether for seed grants or training, should be available to all faculty regardless of rank. Some called this unrealistic for higher education. I just called it equitable access.

These testimonials are illustrative of the resource implications of a two-tiered faculty system based on status differentials that permeate institutional practices and administrative priorities. As Purcell further notes, central to NTT status is the stigma of secondary faculty status:[4]

> It is the stigma of assumed professional failure, and it is the result of a pernicious illusion: that of the academic meritocracy. Those who enjoy the privilege of the tenure track, this illusion presumes, have earned their place by their merit. They have been vetted and found worthy. Non-tenure tracks, by contrast, have not been vetted; they are undeserving. Their presence in the department, according to this logic, is illegitimate, inappropriate, transgressive.

Given the often unspoken yet underlying stigma attached to NTT status, even the obvious first step of raising awareness about inequitable contingent faculty practices cannot be taken for granted. Consider in this regard a study involving forty members of higher education stakeholder groups. As the study found, just raising awareness of the inefficiency of NTT practices in relation to the overall health of the academic profession could be a factor that facilitates change.[5] Arguably, such awareness should be obvious, and change strategies need to build on this awareness to emphasize benefits to the institution that address long-term educational interests.

In addressing the power of status differentials, the description of contingent faculty as "invisible" by Judith Gappa and David Leslie underscores the urgency and necessity of a reconceived employment relationship.[6] The model for change needs to incorporate key elements of social exchange theory in refashioning the contract between contingent faculty and the institution. Social exchange theory emphasizes the reciprocity of the economic and social contract between the individual and the employer.[7] The concepts of equity and fairness, or what is termed "organizational justice," are particularly relevant in terms of whether contingent faculty perceive that the organization has treated them fairly.[8]

With the concept of reciprocity at the forefront, we build on the contingent faculty framework of Judith Gappa, Ann Austin, and Andrea Trice in *Rethinking Faculty Work* (2007). This framework posits the need for five essential aspects of faculty work that are founded on a bedrock of respect: employment equity, academic freedom and autonomy, collegiality and community involvement, balance and flexibility, and professional growth.[9] Reciprocity, or the term "reciprocal empowerment" that we have used in prior research, involves a shifting in the locus of asymmetrical power relationships and ultimately a sharing of power. Reciprocal empowerment involves three primary components: collaboration and democratic participation, such as in academic planning and faculty governance; self-determination in cultures of dignity and inclusion; and distributive justice in terms of opportunity and total rewards structures.[10] Note that these elements have particular import for members of marginalized groups who may be silenced, ignored, and even undercut in their professional endeavors.[11]

What will be the long-term consequences of disaffection with working conditions by contingent faculty? We have certainly seen the increasing shift toward unionization as the only viable pathway for contingent faculty seeking to ameliorate the terms and conditions of employment. As our interviewees have pointed out, inadequate compensation, lack of benefits, and insecure working conditions mean that only a certain segment of the academic population can afford to take adjunct positions or even in some cases full-time contingent faculty positions. Recall Andrea's keen observation that higher education is at a turning point when adverse pay and working conditions will mean that only rich housewives will be able to hold adjunct positions. Similarly, Viviana, the Southeast Asian adjunct faculty member cited earlier, observes that only people who have other sources of income can afford to teach at her elite university in adjunct roles. These working conditions preclude individuals with lower incomes from teaching and necessarily limit socioeconomic diversity:

> I think the people who are adjuncts here all have jobs or have other sources of income; they do it for love of topic. I mean, I don't think anybody does it to make a living, because I cannot imagine that anybody could withstand the insecurity of not knowing whether they're going to have enough enrollment for the course, because there's always like some minimum threshold of enrollment or otherwise the course is canceled. . . . How could anybody count on paying bills with that, right? So, I feel like most people I run into who are adjuncts have full-time jobs or means by which they can do this, and they do it for love of topic and engagement. . . . When you're looking at diversity, you're not getting income diversity, you're not getting people who could be fabulous.

THE URGENT NEED FOR CULTURAL CHANGE

The double marginalization that minoritized contingent faculty may experience within their departmental or school cultures adds to the precariousness of their status. In the largely decentralized environment of higher education, departmental cultures can vary significantly in terms of microclimates and the degree of inclusion. For the most part, the expectation for minoritized contingent faculty is that they must alter modes of behavior and expectations to fit normative cultural expectations. The larger question remains, however, as to how institutional and departmental cultures can change so that the onus is not on minoritized faculty to adapt.

While formal practices for contingent faculty usually fall under the purview of the office of the provost, considerable variation exists in the operationalization of these practices within departments and schools.

Research conducted by Adrianna Kezar with a sample of 107 NTT faculty in twenty-five departments at three master's-level institutions found a continuum consisting of four distinct types of departmental cultures in relation to contingent faculty. The study has also yielded a valuable self-assessment tool on departmental cultures and NTT faculty developed through the Delphi Project on the Changing Faculty and Student Success at the University of Southern California. The four cultural types range from destructive to learning cultures:[12]

1. *Destructive cultures,* in which NTT faculty perceive disrespect and hostility from tenured faculty and are not given the resources or opportunities necessary for their success;
2. *Neutral or invisible cultures,* in which NTT faculty are treated as temporary faculty or simply the delivery mechanisms for course content;
3. *Inclusive cultures,* in which NTT faculty are recognized as professionals, but policies and practices do not reflect their contributions to the learning environment; and
4. *Learning cultures,* in which NTT faculty are treated as professional equals with tenure-rank faculty and included in faculty meetings and professional opportunities.

The first two types of cultures in this spectrum are characterized by inequitable salaries and working conditions, while inclusive cultures are characterized by attempts to create some alignment between contingent and tenured faculty compensation practices. As revealed in this study, adjuncts experienced the most negative working conditions in destructive and neutral cultures, while full-time contingent faculty in the same environment at least had the benefit of relationships that gave them some protection against these conditions. Finally, in a learning environment, department chairs actively seek to provide equitable salaries and benefits for NTT faculty. Nonetheless, these terms and conditions are necessarily governed in many instances by institutional policy and resource allocations.

Due to the enormous variation in institutional types, missions, and geographic locations, contingent faculty practices are also heavily influenced by institutional context and the prevailing educational environment. These differences necessarily arise based on the mission of a college or university and the institution's geographic location and demographic makeup and even on the political leanings and influence of state legislatures in a given state. In recent days, the impact of politically charged environments within some states and the passage of prohibitive state legislation related to diversity training clearly has had significant ripple effects within college classrooms. Cultural change in these environments can be a decidedly uphill battle.

To discuss the impact of environmental pressures on institutional culture and practices, we explore further the impact of a highly polarized national climate for diversity in the United States on the experiences of minoritized contingent faculty.

THE DIVISIVE CLIMATE FOR DIVERSITY

In a time of deep racial polarization within the United States, the work environment for minoritized contingent faculty has become even more precarious. Following a wave of protests in 2020 and 2021 against police brutality in the killing of unarmed Black citizens including George Floyd in Minneapolis, Breonna Taylor in Louisville, Rayshard Brooks in Atlanta, and Daunte Wright in Minneapolis, it seemed as if the United States might come to a racial reckoning and explore the consequences of 246 years (1619–1865) of a slavery-based economic system characterized by systemic racism.[13] But pushback by President Donald Trump in his Executive Order 13950 of September 2020 titled "Combatting Race and Sex Stereotyping" resulted in a ban on diversity training in federal agencies and for federal contractors that involved "divisive concepts" suggesting "that the United States is fundamentally racist or sexist." This antidemocratic executive order sent a rapid chill through corporate America, academia, and governmental agencies.[14] The order contained language indicating that diversity training should not cause discomfort or stress to any individual related to his or her race or gender, should not imply that individuals act implicitly or unconsciously in racist or sexist ways, and should not suggest that concepts of meritocracy and hard work are racist or sexist.[15] Perhaps less well known is the influence of conservative activist Christopher Rufo in the formulation of Trump's executive order through his spin campaign against so-called critical race theory (CRT).

During the pandemic, meetings on Zoom were often recorded and became readily accessible to the public. When an employee of the City of Seattle sent documentation from an antibias training session to Rufo, he immediately saw the political opportunity it offered. Rufo found CRT to be a powerful political weapon, believing that the term "connotes hostile, academic, divisive, race-obsessed, poisonous, elitist, anti-American" views.[16] In an appearance on September 2, 2020, on Tucker Carlson's Fox news program, Rufo called on President Trump to issue an executive order against CRT-related training: "Conservatives need to wake up. This is an existential threat to the United States." Rufo was immediately contacted by Mark Meadows, Trump's chief of staff, and summoned to Washington, DC, to help draft the executive order. Let us step back to understand the misappropriation of CRT by Rufo and others who view CRT as emblematic of a Marxist strain and their potent use of this semantic umbrella to attack antiracism and diversity training as a whole. In fact, CRT is a legal theory that arose in the mid-1970 by scholars who sought to examine how race, power, and US law intersect within the larger economic, legal, and social context. These scholars recognized the importance of the law in civil rights reform as well as how lawful practices had codified disadvantages and privileges through legal segregation and other discriminatory practices.[17] Although some variations in the humanities and social science have emerged in CRT scholarship, these theorists recognize that racism in the United States is not aberrational but instead is imbued with "ordinariness" and affects the everyday experiences of people of color. CRT scholars also see race as social construction without biological or genetic reality. And as Derrick Bell, the first tenured Black professor at Harvard Law School, recognized, progressive civil rights protests such as those in the 1960s will be more likely to bring about change when they converge with other interests that are differently motivated.[18]

Yet, the furor over CRT tapped into a deep vein of white racial anxiety about the changing demographics of the United States and increasing numbers of underrepresented students in school classrooms.[19] Even though President Joe Biden rescinded the executive order immediately after assuming office in 2021, Republican-led state legislatures began closely emulating the language of the executive order in legislative actions patterned after Trump's regressive edict and introduced bills or took related steps to restrict teaching related to racial equity, white privilege, and so-called divisive concepts under what was termed "critical race theory." By January 2021, eighteen states had enacted such measures designed to restrict or limit how teachers can discuss racism and sexism.[20] These new laws amount to censorship and possible violation of the intent of the First and Fourteenth Amendments.

Consider also the impact on the nation when on January 6, 2021, a violent mob of mostly white supporters of Trump invaded and attacked the US Capitol in an insurrection designed to stop the certification of the votes by the House of Representatives for President-elect Joe Biden. Egged on by a speech given by Trump urging them to show strength, rioters paraded through the Capitol halls bearing Confederate flags, while outside other Trump supporters shouted racial slurs at Black Capitol police officers and set up gallows and nooses reminiscent of the lynchings of Black Americans.[21] In a speech marking the tenth anniversary of the Martin Luther King Jr. memorial in Washington, DC, on October 21, 2021, President Biden stated, "The violent, deadly insurrection on the Capitol nine months ago, it was about white supremacy, in my opinion."[22]

Following violent episodes such as the attack on the Capitol, Dominic, a Latinx male contingent sociology faculty member at a southwestern university, described how he has had to pull back and exercise more care about what he says in the classroom:

> But once those divisions started to have violent connotations to them and even violent manifestations like we saw on January 6, I started self-policing a bit. And I know that I'm not the only one, especially as since 2016 more and more attacks on immigrants in the Latino community [have occurred] and when you vocalize even general criticisms of, let's say, ICE [Immigration and Customs Enforcement]. These are criticisms that I had been discussing for well over a decade. But I felt that I was going to get more student pushback, and I would be much more likely to receive attention on social media groups like Facebook groups; on our campus we have groups that do monitor the lectures and of course media presented by faculty[,] . . . and they talk about what I talked about in class.

Furthermore, with the advent of the pandemic and the switch to online courses recorded on Zoom and other media, the content of lectures can be quickly shared on the internet. The rapidity of communication on social media platforms can create an immediate backlash when discussions in class are taken out of context. In this regard, Dominic explains how student and alumni groups on and off campus have connections with powerful individuals in the university hierarchy all the way up to the chancellor and that comments and discussions can be quickly magnified or distorted. As a result, Dominic must consider carefully issues he chooses to address in the classroom even when he expects that students might benefit from more robust discussions. As he explains,

These are students and alumni, and just with the, as they call it, "concerned citizens,"... are very aware of what we are discussing, and the unfortunate reality is that these groups do have the ears of powerful individuals from ... the Board of Regents even all the way up to the chancellor's office, and it would be silly of me to think that that's not the case. So, for example, ... we moved our classes online last year, and I was recording them and then posting them online, very exposed. ... It felt like ... these people ... aren't looking to contextualize what I'm saying into a larger story or the whole class. They'll see one piece of one lecture and be like "clearly this guy is unfit; he's just an example of why we need to get rid of [him]," and it snowballs.

As a result, given his minoritized status and lack of tenure protection, Dominic has had to avoid discussion of controversial issues that could jeopardize his employment even when he believes that such discussions could benefit the students:

And the problem is that even though I know that it's pedagogically sound and it could be beneficial to the students, I will not do it because I fear the potential backlash that could come my way. I fear that part of it is because I am an instructional faculty member—I don't have the protection of tenure—but also because people will hear my name ... [and] they'll know that I'm a Latino professor, they'll know that I am a sociology professor, and even people that can't even spell "sociology" will be like "you know those people," and they'll combine it with a phrase I put out there or a word I said, and that's it. It doesn't need to go any farther than that [and] becomes the story. And I can easily be dismissed because I have no ultimate protection here.

Similarly, Justin, the Black male clinical professor in an elite private university cited earlier, indicates that since the election of Donald Trump, he has had to be more on his guard in the classroom because of what he calls a "deterioration" in the environment. This claustrophobic atmosphere has led Justin for the first time to describe a situation in which he now feels that he can't breathe. As he indicates, "I've never felt that I couldn't breathe, until now.... It's a constant weathering that's occurring." The stifling effect of the current national atmosphere has affected his creativity and even his desire to write about what he is experiencing because he is living it. Justin describes the administrative warning sent out by his previous dean right after Trump's election that made "the tides become rougher" in the classroom:

> It was right after the election of Trump that we received emails from our previous dean.... In class discussions, we have to become more open to conservative viewpoints and to allow conservatives to feel comfortable within the classroom. And it created this whole conversation of "well, that's what we do anyway for all people, but we also challenge individuals who may have ... false narratives or false states with empirical research or with facts, just facts." And we were getting this pushback: "Be careful. They deserve space to be heard." So, even if they're talking about the eradication of immigrants from our country, do we allow that space?

Given the highly contentious climate for diversity, minoritized contingent faculty have experienced a chill and a reverberation emanating from national and state developments. Take, for example, the veritable tsunami of measures rapidly introduced by Republican governor Ron DeSantis and the highly conservative Republican legislature in Florida to ban the teaching of CRT and diversity-related concepts in public schools and defund DEI programs in public colleges and universities. DeSantis has criticized what he terms "the woke class" in which he believes students learn to hate each other,[23] and both he and the legislature have evinced clear hostility to diversity. First, in June 2021 the Florida Board of Education banned the teaching of CRT from public school classrooms. DeSantis appeared at the board meeting by video to encourage the members, many of whom were his appointees, to take this measure that he indicated would provide students with facts rather than "trying to indoctrinate them with ideology."[24] Then in September 2021, Representative Randy Fine from Palm Bay introduced House Bill 57 titled "Racial and Sexual Discrimination," a wide-ranging legislative effort patterned after Trump's Executive Order 13950 designed to curtail diversity, inclusion, and critical race-related training that espouses certain concepts in all public and state institutions.[25] The bill later died, however, in the Education and Employment Committee in 2022.

Not content with the broad language of House Bill 57, Governor DeSantis introduced sweeping legislation called "Stop the Wrongs to Our Kids and Employees" and dubbed the "Stop WOKE Act" in December 2021. This bill, signed by DeSantis in April 2022, allows parents to sue schools for teaching CRT and prevents school funding for consultants connected to CRT. This bill was modeled after the Texas antiabortion law allowing private citizens to sue anyone who assists in an abortion after six weeks. The Florida legislation also precludes staff from taking antiracist therapy or training. Remarkably, when introducing his bill, DeSantis quoted Reverend Martin Luther King's statement about not judging people by the color of their skin but by the content of their character. DeSantis further linked the push for racial equity in schools as a distortion of history: "Just to understand, when you hear 'equity' used, that is just an ability for people to smuggle in their ideology. We don't need to have those terms."[26]

Moving further to restrict classroom discussions in schools, in March 2022 Governor DeSantis signed the "Parental Rights in Education" law, which has been dubbed the "don't say gay" law. This law prohibits discussion of sexual orientation and gender identity in kindergarten through third grade "or in a manner that is not age appropriate or developmentally appropriate for students in accordance with state standards." The vague language of the law could be interpreted to limit discussion of gender and sexuality in all grades.[27] In May 2023, the Florida Board of Education expanded the ban on discussion of sexual orientation and gender identity in public schools to grades four through twelve unless such discussion is part of reproductive health instruction that students can elect to take. The stifling of academic discussion involving diversity-related concepts led to further efforts to curtail academic freedom in the higher education environment. For example, a the University of Florida, the state's flagship public research university, a grievance was filed by the faculty union regarding pressures by academic administration to remove the word "critical" when paired with "race" from a new doctoral concentration in education titled "Critical Study of Race, Ethnicity, and Culture in Education." The associate provost cited the political realities in the State of Florida, and in a separate meeting the dean of the college of education encouraged the faculty to read HB 57.[28]

Governor DeSantis's explicit attack on DEI programs further expanded to public colleges and universities in May 2023 with the signing of S.B. 266, prohibiting the spending of federal and state funds on programs that "advocate for diversity, equity, and inclusion, or promote or engage in political or social activism." Limited exceptions to this law include programs or functions required for compliance with federal law or for maintaining discipline-specific accreditation.[29] In a remarkable attempt to placate DeSantis, in January 2023 the presidents of twenty-eight community colleges signed a statement indicating that their institutions would not "fund or support any institutional practice, policy, or academic requirement that compels belief in critical race theory or related concepts such as intersectionality, or the idea that systems of oppression should be the primary lens through which teaching and learning are analyzed and/or improved upon."[30] In January 2023, the American Association of University Professors convened a special committee "to review an apparent pattern of politically, racially, and ideologically motivated attacks on public higher education in Florida." Following interviews with professors across the state, the preliminary findings issued on May 23, 2023, identify a systematic effort by the governor and the state legislature "to dictate and enforce conformity with a narrow and reactionary political and ideological agenda throughout the state's higher education system." The report notes that a central feature of this agenda has been the effort to undermine and eliminate from college and university programs "ideas and information about race, gender, and sexual identity that fail to conform to the prejudices of politicians."[31] The treacherous nature of the contested political environment for DEI means that minoritized contingent faculty must be on their guard in raising controversial issues that could jeopardize their employment status. Even when leaders of color such as deans raise diversity issues, they can be perceived through a stereotypical lens as angry or oversensitive. Carolyn Hodges and Olga Welch, two Black female deans, point out that

> the resistance we faced caused a feeling of being under surveillance, especially when people charged us with being too angry or oversensitive, when we were simply offering a viewpoint counter to the status quo or dared to point out racial inequities. These responses of resistance and reticence constituted a form of institutional gaslighting, suggesting that we had overstepped our boundaries and perhaps even insulted their efforts meant to instill diversity and inclusion and to remove any suggestion of institutional racism. In such instances, instead of being a partner to that struggle, persons of color become ungrateful guests.[32]

If even deans can be subjected to this type of gaslighting and exclusionary mistreatment, it is clear that minoritized contingent faculty must be even more on their guard. The crushing of scholarly discussion on race, class, sexual orientation, gender identity, and other controversial issues in higher education controverts the aims of academy to foster critical thinking and promote research. The American Association of University Professors' "Statement on Legislation Restricting Teaching about Race" underscores the dangers of political interference in higher education that undermine the mission of colleges and universities and the student educational process. Ideological restrictions on discussion of the role of race in US history "also severely violate both academic freedom, the cornerstone of American higher education and the faculty's primary role in institutional decision-making."

SIGNS OF HOPE?

The breadth and scope of the shift in the academic landscape over the last half century argues for a reformulation of the entire talent framework for contingent faculty rather than a merely piecemeal look at change.[33] From a broad perspective, one of the first conditions for change in creating a more diverse and inclusive workplace for contingent faculty is the need for a comprehensive talent strategy focused on recruitment, hiring, professional development, retention, and total rewards. The recalibration of the contingent faculty total rewards strategy encompasses monetary compensation as well as nonfinancial rewards including benefits, professional advancement, career development, and work/life balance.

The lack of attention to a significant body of human resources research in establishing equity in structural working conditions for contingent faculty represents a rather startling disconnect. Just as one example, Michael Crow and William Dabars's book *Designing the New American University* (2015) does not even address structural inequality in faculty employment or discuss contingent faculty practices.[34] This omission suggests that the excessive supply of PhD candidates in the academic job market has led to complacency in terms of contingent faculty talent practices by institutions of higher education. This short-sighted expectation appears to take the excessive supply of PhDs interested in contingent work as a constant by assuming that individuals will continue to be willing to work at minimal salary levels without career stability for indefinite time periods. But the great resignation occurring during the

COVID-19 pandemic that resulted in 4.4 million, or 3 percent, of the US workforce quitting their jobs in September 2021 alone suggests that the situation could change as individuals seek other career paths that offer greater stability and rewards.[35]

Recent research in human resources emphasizes the quality of the employee experience throughout the employment life cycle as key to retention and job satisfaction. Organizations are shifting the focus from employee engagement to the employee experience, beginning with onboarding and continuing throughout the career cycle. From this perspective, employee experience is the lever that will impact individuals' discretionary commitment and the willingness to go above and beyond in contributing to organizational goals. Ultimately, practices that emphasize the employee experience contribute positively to organizational performance and financial success. As one survey of public and private companies with 1,820 respondents found that when human resources functions foster a positive employee experience, respondents were 1.3 times more likely to report organizational outperformance.[36]

The pandemic may have, however, begun to shift the higher education employment scales in favor of change. Dr. Robert Sellers, vice provost for equity and inclusion and chief diversity officer at the University of Michigan, indicates that the disruption caused by the pandemic can lead institutions to rethink how they deliver curricula and create greater alignment between the working conditions of tenure-track and contingent faculty. As he explains,

> I am hopeful that with a disruption as large as we've had [comes] the opportunity to really rethink in some fundamental ways how we deliver curricula in higher education, that we will take advantage of the sort of potential sea change to do so in ways that are more equitable across the board in a number of different ways. Not only in terms of . . . social identities but also around occupations and labels, the contingent faculty versus noncontingent.

Given the impact of the pandemic's disruption, Sellers sees the potential for greater convergence of structures for contingent faculty with the tenured ranks. He envisions a broadening of opportunities for promotion stability and cites the further development of programs already under way at the University of Michigan that cut across the ranks of tenured and contingent faculty, including professional development opportunities, recognition and support programs, and leadership development. An example of this convergence at the university is the implementation of a climate survey that collects data specific to contingent faculty experiences and is leading to the development of college and school reports to address the findings. Other examples include a summer initiative on inclusive pedagogy with the Center for Research on Teaching and Learning in which the university has partnered with the lecturers' union to provide between eight to ten slots for this learning opportunity. In addition, the university has a membership in the National Center for Faculty Development and Diversity, which covers all faculty regardless of contingent or tenure status.

In thinking about the change process, Sellers notes that anecdotally he has been amazed by the commitment of contingent faculty as champions of change, despite the precariousnature of their positions. Like staff, they have the most to lose, but in his words, they "are willing to step up, to speak up," and even "step out in ways that some of the tenured faculty have been less willing to do." Sellers presciently notes both the oppression faced by minoritized faculty in general and the privilege relative to others that he holds based on tenured status. He finds it important not to let oppression "become more salient" and "blind individuals from the privilege they also hold." Awareness of both privilege and oppression can provide the necessary ballast in advocating for institutional change.

In the same vein as Mark Purcell points out, the academic hierarchy subconsciously reinforces the sense of privilege among tenured faculty and belief in the meritocracy of the system. Once having attained tenure, one can forget what it was like to be a contingent faculty member who has to worry about employment on a daily basis. Since attaining tenure and having left the uncertainty of contingent faculty status, Purcell candidly indicates that he's "lost that ability to remember what it's like every day of not knowing what's going to happen next year." He also notes from personal experience that contingent faculty can tend to blame themselves for their secondary status:

> And I have had several faculty that I am close to, and I have tried . . . to reiterate constantly . . . your position is not due to your failings; it's not due to your shortcomings. That person didn't get that job because they're better than you. . . . They got lucky; it's roulette wheel stuff. . . . There's a whole group of people we're talking about who do deserve [a tenure-track position], and there's no space for them. . . . But what else do people think when they don't get a job? There must be something wrong with me.

In the face of severe budgetary constraints particularly in public higher education, Purcell proposes the reallocation of security as a material resource that would benefit contingent faculty. Currently, employment security is given through what Purcell calls "nuclear security," virtually lifetime employment for tenured faculty and provided only in very limited measure to contingent faculty. Emergence of the teaching category of ladder faculty offers a greater degree of security and, although not a perfect solution, provides a viable avenue to help bridge the distance between tenured and contingent ranks. Such reallocation, Purcell emphasizes, would require peer review every three to five years to ensure continued effective performance including for post-tenure faculty. This reallocation would distribute both the security and the risks when coupled with the capability of critical evaluation throughout the whole career. As he states, "you have provisions that make you secure, and we also have the capability as a group to do critical evaluation of your work and make sure it's still the kind of work that your department needs."

CONCLUSION

The highly inequitable and unstable working conditions for adjunct faculty as well as some full-time contingent faculty have made it nearly impossible for many individuals without other income streams to assume adjunct faculty positions and even some full-time contingent roles. Recall Viviana's statement that these working conditions eliminate talented individuals without alternative means and preclude greater diversity in the contingent ranks. In her words, "Most people I run into who are adjuncts have full-time jobs or means by which they can do this, and they do it for love of topic and engagement. . . . When you're looking at diversity, you're not getting income diversity, you're not getting people who could be fabulous."

The experiences of minoritized contingent faculty reflected in this book illustrate the double jeopardy faced by these faculty due to their uncertain employment status and the marginalization and differential expectations that can occur based on their social identities. With the potential for nonrenewal as a continuous consideration, these faculty can encounter significant pushback in the classroom when discussing controversial subjects that can jeopardize their employment status. The conservative raft of state laws precluding the teaching of so-called divisive concepts including racial equity, white privilege, and CRT has stifling effects on minoritized contingent faculty in the classroom. As our interviewees note, the increase in virulent, openly white supremacist speech with attendant violent connotations has created the need for even greater caution by minoritized faculty. With the advent of Zoom classes that are often recorded, their statements can be amplified, and student complaints can ratchet up to the highest administrative levels, creating a situation of vulnerability for minoritized contingent faculty. And as we have also seen, the geographic location of the college or university and the political dynamics within a given state have a significant impact on the teaching environment.

Given the current perilous political environment for minoritized contingent faculty, in chapter 6 we will examine specific policy and practice approaches undertaken by universities and colleges that can lead to a more inclusive culture and improved working conditions.

6

Moving the Needle in Contingent Faculty Employment: Recommendations for Change

Faculty working conditions are student learning conditions.

AMERICAN ASSOCIATION OF UNIVERSITY
PROFESSORS, "BACKGROUND FACTS ON
CONTINGENT FACULTY POSITIONS"

The overreliance on contingent faculty as the primary purveyor of the teaching of undergraduate college students in many research universities is nothing short of catastrophic for the future of higher education. Contingent faculty now play a vital yet largely unrewarded role in making the functioning of universities possible. With only one-third of the faculty now in tenure-line positions, contingent faculty have become the essential frontline workers of higher education. Terms such as "academic sharecroppers," "Uber drivers," and "Walmart workers" now thread the literature to describe the mistreatment of adjuncts in particular.[1] For example, Kaia Shivers, clinical assistant professor at New York University, describes adjuncts as "the fast food, Walmart workers of higher education," with students as "the casualties of corporatized education."[2]

The devaluation of teaching by delegation to an academic underclass has significant and far-reaching ramifications for students and the educational process itself. The subpar working conditions of many contingent faculty can limit their ability to address student needs and provide a high-quality educational environment. Through no fault of their own, contingent faculty may not be able to share fully their talents, knowledge, and creativity whether in or outside the classroom.[3] Research has shown a relationship between increases in part-time faculty and a decline in graduation and retention rates.[4] The precariousness of nontenured faculty employment can impact student learning and success and undermine the core educational mission of universities and colleges. Our narratives reveal the heavy workloads of contingent faculty, who are often teaching large sections, grading papers, mentoring students, and holding office hours with little time or support for research. Recall the story of Gila Berryman, a Black English adjunct at the New York City College of Technology who felt like a fraud when teaching her minoritized students the skills needed to obtain employment while she herself was forced into a subsistence existence on food stamps.[5] Without benefits and job security, eking out a subsistence existence through adjunct employment sends the wrong message about how higher education treats its faculty and, by extension, its students. Most significantly, espoused institutional values of equity and inclusion are not reflected in such disparate employment realities.

As highlighted in chapter 1, the marked decline in state funding for higher education by conservative legislatures has been linked to partisan affiliations related to racial identity and correlated with rising student diversity. If present trends continue, the budgetary horizon for public higher education remains bleak, with state funding potentially reaching zero by 2059. The largest growth in adjunctification has occurred in public institutions, particularly doctoral institutions. With 14.6 million of the nation's 19.7 million students enrolled in public institutions, lack of support for public higher education disproportionately impacts students of color and low-income students. Much more needs to be done by top academic leaders in lobbying state legislatures to counteract the current trend.

How can colleges and universities begin to instigate long-needed change in contingent faculty policies and build more inclusive talent practices for minoritized non-tenure-track (NTT) faculty? Surprisingly,

John Cross and Edie Goldenberg's 2009 study of ten prominent public and private research universities found that top academic administrators including presidents, provosts, and deans were not well informed on the status of NTT faculty and tended to underestimate the number of such faculty, particularly when different titles were used.[6] That the highest-ranking academic administrators would lack knowledge about the two-tiered faculty system seems highly implausible. Perhaps since 2009, greater awareness of the contingent faculty workforce has permeated the upper echelons of higher education, particularly in light of the widespread layoffs of these faculty in public universities.

In this chapter we will share a number of recommendations that can create the opportunity for ongoing transformational change in contingent faculty practices. These change processes necessarily involve substantial organizational redesign, systematic phase-based planning, significant budgetary reassessment, collaboration with key stakeholder groups, and sustained institutional commitment from the top.

SECURE COMMITMENT FROM THE PRESIDENT AND THE PROVOST TO UNDERTAKE A MAJOR REVIEW

A critical step in transforming contingent faculty practices is to secure commitment from the president and the provost to undertake a major review and work with faculty governance bodies in the process. Consider the experiences of Marla, a Latina administrator who served as the chief diversity officer in a major private university. Marla left the role, discouraged that she could not undertake, among many goals, structural changes that would address the overall well-being of contingent faculty, particularly since she found inequity in the way these roles tend to be highly gendered and racialized. Marla felt shut down. "The way I experienced it—I had a clear idea of what I wanted to get done." But her role was diminished into more of a secretarial/support role to other agendas, and she was virtually told to "stay in your lane, you are not authorized, focus on the work of the office" without acknowledging that this was the work of her office. As a result, Marla did not have the space or support to meaningfully engage in changing the working conditions of the contingent faculty.

Marla observes, as we have also noted, that most institutions of higher education have a very strong hierarchy that usually lacks racial and gender diversity. As a result, the diversity office is frequently underresourced while tasked with serving a broad constituency of faculty, staff, students, alumni, and the community. Marla's vision for this work was to create a philosophical approach and policy alternatives that, as she puts it, "would end the continued exploitation of the vulnerable." Since the contingent faculty ranks will likely be the most significant area for faculty growth in the future, the need to make sure these jobs are secure is a priority.

In contrast, take the systematic approach to structural changes in NTT policies undertaken at Worcester Polytechnic Institute, a private university focused on engineering and technical education over the course of a decade. Initial changes to NTT policies were enacted between 2009 and 2012 to standardize evaluation processes, hiring protocols, promotion criteria, and titling for contingent faculty. Then based on a 2019 report, Worcester Polytechnic Institute's faculty governance worked with a newly formed NTT faculty council and the provost to develop a three-pronged approach that would strengthen the working conditions of full-time contingent faculty. First, they formulated a tenure pathway for 40 percent of the teaching faculty, proposed long-term contracts for all full-time contingent faculty, and included NTT faculty in governance processes. In 2021, all three major changes were approved by the faculty and subsequently by the president, the provost, and the board of trustees in 2021. In August 2021, the first fifteen teaching faculty were appointed to the tenure track. Particularly notable in this example is the formation of an NTT faculty council and work with faculty governance in developing a long-term approach to structural inequality. A comprehensive change management plan will involve the mapping of phases with timelines and expected outcomes for each phase.[7]

RETHINK THE ROLE OF HUMAN RESOURCES
IN CONTINGENT FACULTY PRACTICES

Because the organization itself and its design have been shown to have three to four times more effect on performance compared with individual contributions,[8] this recommendation focuses on how institutions can leverage the untapped capabilities of the HR department in the development of contingent faculty talent practices. Colleges and universities have not kept pace with workforce trends in private industry that have established the value of strategic HR practices in organizational success.[9] With the rapid changes occurring in the higher education environment due to COVID-19 and increased budgetary constraints, the redesign of contingent faculty talent processes will benefit from strategic HR principles. To further mission-related values of equity and consistency in employment practices, systematic application of research-based HR constructs to the processes of recruitment, hiring, compensation, total rewards, employee relations, and professional development will benefit universities and colleges in the design and development of a more inclusive talent proposition.

Yet, for the most part HR departments in higher education have been overlooked in the development and implementation of practices and policies for contingent faculty. HR is often siloed under the umbrella of the finance division, an area with a significantly different focus and knowledge base and different responsibilities and goals. This anomalous positioning of HR fails to actualize the competencies, knowledge, and skills of HR professionals in the areas of change management and talent practices. Unlike private industry where the chief HR officer typically reports to the CEO and serves on the executive staff, HR in higher education is sidelined and significantly underutilized.[10] At doctoral institutions, chief HR officers typically report to the chief business officer (35 percent) or chief financial officer (19 percent), with only 20 percent of chief HR officers reporting directly to the president/chancellor. This pattern is largely similar at master's and baccalaureate institutions.[11] These reporting relationships have basically not shifted over the last decade.

In most colleges and universities, HR's areas of responsibility center exclusively on staff functions with the exception of benefits, retirement, certain aspects of faculty professional development, and payroll. While the provost's office may contain an academic personnel unit, this unit typically focuses specifically on promotion and tenure processes, faculty labor relations and negotiation, position control, budget, and academically related payroll functions. Based on its current focus and portfolio of responsibilities, HR is often viewed as a more bureaucratic, transactionally oriented organization rather than as consultants and facilitators. In some cases, HR's role in regulatory issues and policy compliance has overshadowed its role as strategic partner. Further, HR professionals can be viewed by academicians as lacking the knowledge, professional expertise, and competencies needed for faculty functions.[12]

An extensive body of research developed through seven global rounds of data gathering by Dave Ulrich, Wayne Brockbank, and other scholars at the University of Michigan indicates that the evolution of a strategic HR architecture requires four critical factors: alignment with mission and stakeholder needs, development of strategic HR competencies, creation and realization of organizational capabilities, and a design and structure that serve organizational needs.[13]

Let us consider these factors individually and their implications for HR in the implementation of inclusive contingent employment practices. First, alignment with academic mission and stakeholder needs involves a repositioning of HR within the institution to ensure that HR has a seat at the table through reexamination of its reporting relationship and its ability to participate in organizational decision-making. As talent strategists, HR can contribute research-based approaches to institution-wide issues and gather input from stakeholders to help shape and reach desired outcomes. At the same time, HR professionals need to be equipped with the expertise and knowledge of academic matters and access to the resources that will help them assume this expanded role.[14]

Second, strategic HR competencies that will help in the delivery of value in contingent faculty processes include the following:[15]

Culture and change champion, integrating change initiatives into the over-all culture change process.

Human capital curator, facilitating the flow of talent through the career cycle. Given the decentralized nature of many employment processes, HR can create value in its work with divisions and departments to maximize talent capacity.

Total rewards steward, promoting equity and well-being through financial and nonfinancial rewards including compensation, benefits, professional development, recognition programs, and work/life and well-being initiatives.

These three strategic competencies each necessarily involve DEI in their realization.

Organizational capabilities represent the collective abilities of an organization to implement its strategy and create value for its stakeholders. These capabilities differentiate and define the identity of an organization, since they permeate organizational culture. Based on 2016 data, Ulrich and others have identified eleven basic capabilities that affect organizational performance and are grouped in three categories: innovation, speed, and human capital. The human capital capabilities are talent, leadership, accountability, and operational efficiency.[16] Further, one of the capabilities included under innovation is culture or shared mindset. All of these capabilities can be marshaled to support changes in contingent faculty working conditions.

Finally, the logic and structure of HR needs to follow the organization's logic and structure as a whole and its overall strategy. While little study has been done on the impact of integrated HR systems in higher education, research from the private sector confirms the impact of high-performance HR systems on organizational performance and financial outcomes.[17] The synergy among HR practices including total rewards, professional development, and recruitment and hiring will enable greater alignment with institutional strategy, allow for a holistic approach to contingent faculty practices, and contribute to enhanced organizational performance.

The role of HR in the design and development of integrated practices for contingent faculty can range from compensation structures, career ladders, and professional development to work/life and recognition programs.

ENSURE THAT DIVERSITY STRATEGIC PLANS ADDRESS THE INCLUSION OF MINORITIZED CONTINGENT FACULTY

A third major recommendation is to ensure that diversity strategic plans specifically address contingent faculty and also include specific initiatives directed toward the inclusion of minoritized contingent faculty. Notably, as universities and colleges showcase their faculty diversity initiatives extensively through written plans on the internet, little mention is made of initiatives for contingent faculty. Searching for the words "adjunct" and "contingent" in many such diversity strategic plans typically yields no results, while there are often many references to tenure-line faculty. This glaring omission underscores the invisibility of contingent faculty, despite statements related to inclusive excellence that refer to the values of quality and diversity in higher education. Further, in large institutions, separate DEI plans for schools and colleges may vary significantly in their focus and whether contingent faculty issues are addressed. The inconsistency of approaches to contingent faculty practices even within a single institution is a matter of concern.

The lack of attention to the disparate structure of contingent faculty employment is evident even in large-scale diversity plans. At most, passing reference is made to strengthening hiring and outreach processes for adjunct positions to foster greater diversity and offer increased opportunities for full-time employment. Alignment of hiring with affirmative action goals is an often unmet objective. To remedy this situation, partnership between HR and the chief diversity officer and school diversity officers will ensure that goals related to inclusion of minoritized contingent faculty are included in the formal diversity planning process.

IN CONCERT WITH FINANCE AND BUDGET, REVIEW INSTITUTIONAL BUDGET ALLOCATION MODELS FOR NTT FACULTY LINES AND INCREASE SALARIES FOR CONTINGENT FACULTY

One of the most critical priorities for institutions of higher education is to increase the salaries of both part- and full-time contingent faculty and, whenever possible, provide benefits coverage for part-time faculty. Data from a 2019–2020 American Association of University Professors survey indicate that on average, part-time faculty earn $3,557 for teaching a three-credit course, and most adjuncts do not receive either retirement or medical benefits.[18] Many colleges and universities have limited adjunct teaching hours to avoid the need to provide health insurance required under the Affordable Care Act.

While the oversupply of PhDs has allowed the perpetuation of low salaries, it is not a given that this supply will remain constant or that the quality of applicants will be sustainable. A strategic framework for financial decision-making in difficult budgetary times is critical in long-term capacity building for organizational change. Tammy Kolbe, professor at the University of Vermont, and Rick Staisloff, the founder of rpk GROUP, a consulting practice, recommend a change of focus from internal institutional demands to external student needs. Rather than giving small amounts of resources to many projects, they suggest making more significant institutional investments that drive mission and student success. In other words, give priority to long-term solutions rather than short-term fixes.[19]

With these insights at the forefront, consideration can be given to reviewing budgetary allocation processes for contingent faculty through methods such as Lean Six Sigma. This structured approach, although developed in manufacturing, can be adapted to higher education, since it is based on quality and continuous improvement principles that are central to accreditation requirements.[20] In recent years, given increased competition and budgetary cutbacks, interest in Lean Six Sigma has

increased and is reflected in a number of academic books and publications.[21] Lean Six Sigma involves five phases—define, measure, analyze,
improve, and control—in order to identify areas for possible process improvement, reduce redundancy, maximize resources, and enhance quality.
This methodology relies on the observations of employees (in this case
contingent faculty) and utilizes cross-functional input such as from departments and divisions to strengthen organizational outcomes.

For example, following the economic downturn of 2008, the Finance
and Business Services Division of Miami University of Ohio adopted
MU-Lean as a business strategy to generate new ideas for resource creation, eliminate waste within administrative processes, and deliver value.
The vision for this ongoing initiative is to ensure that the student experience is the most positive. With this goal in mind, the university created cross-functional process improvement teams led by the Executive
Steering Team that provides direction, monitors program metrics, and
selects projects. Breakthrough objectives identified by MU-Lean include strategies to increase revenue, improve productivity, reduce costs,
and improve customer satisfaction.[22] As of the close of 2021, 1,824 Lean
projects have been completed, with over 2,500 employees trained on
Lean Six Sigma concepts.[23]

RECOGNIZE THE YEARS OF SERVICE THAT PART-TIME FACULTY CONTRIBUTE TO THE INSTITUTION

Recall the situation at the City University of New York in which long-
serving part-time faculty were summarily nonrenewed through a three-
line impersonal email. Similarly, in an article titled "What's It Like to
'Retire from Nowhere,'" Elizabeth Stone, the pseudonym for a sixty-
eight-year-old adjunct, was left in the dark when her appointment was
nonrenewed at a large northeastern state university after twenty-six
years of working in adjunct and staff positions. The university never communicated anything about her status. Would she have email or library

privileges? Would she even receive an emailed thank you or acknowledgment? Would her time working in different departments and offices
count? Would anyone higher up in the university acknowledge that her
teaching career was ending? Stone chose to tell her students, friends, and
acquaintances that she was retiring. This seemed to suffice until someone
asked where she had retired from. Stone muses, "So, where did I retire
from? The real answer to that question is that I retired from my whole,
rich, varied career." Quoting famous lines from the poet T. S. Elliot,
Stone concluded that she had ended her career "not with a bang, but a
whimper," as her name was rapidly erased from the university website.
The lack of recognition of her long-term service is not unusual. Stone
notes that for her it was not about the money, but like many other contingent faculty who devote decades to teaching, she left without "even
the most basic acknowledgment of her work."[24]

ESTABLISH CAREER LADDERS FOR CONTINGENT FACULTY WITH MULTIYEAR CONTRACTS AND THE POTENTIAL FOR ATTAINING CONTINUING STATUS (TENURE)

Earlier in the book, we described the system at the University of California in which lecturers can be appointed as "lecturers with potential for
security of employment" and progress to "lecturers with security of employment," a status comparable to tenure but without comparable compensation. The University of California has two categories of lecturers:
lecturers who do not have security of employment and are covered by the
collective bargaining agreement of the University Council–American
Federation of Teachers and lecturers with security of employment who
are not covered by the union.

In November 2021, a planned strike by thousands of nontenured professors, lecturers, and other faculty members across nine of the ten University of California campuses was canceled after a tentative agreement

was reached with the University Council–American Federation of Teachers. The agreement was described by the union as "transformative and groundbreaking" and followed a battle of over two and a half years that resulted in one of the strongest contracts for contingent faculty in the United States. The contract included job stability for all lecturers with continuing appointments who are not on the security of employment track in the first six years of teaching beginning with a one-year appointment, followed by a two-year appointment and then three-year appointments until the excellence review. The agreement also included a clear pathway to senior continuing lecturer after three successful merit views following each three-year interval, performance increases of at least 3 percent with every appointment, and the right to be reappointed if deemed effective before external candidates are considered. A significant aspect of the agreement was that all lecturers became eligible for four weeks of fully paid leave for bonding with a new child or for family sick care. The contract also included salary increases each year and 9.5 percent raises for the lowest-paid members.[25]

BUILD SYNERGY AMONG TENURED AND NONTENURED FACULTY TO NEGOTIATE CHANGE

Resistance to contingent faculty working conditions will benefit from the collective voices and combined activism of both tenured and nontenured faculty. As Professor Joseph Schwartz of Temple University points out, political solidarity across ranks can solidify resistance to the "casualization" of academic labor that, in turn, threatens the existence of tenured faculty and undermines the quality of undergraduate education. Schwartz cites the meritocratic myths that can be held among tenured academics who fail to recognize that their contingent colleagues—who work in similar subfields and wrote fine dissertations at similar institutions—are terribly underpaid for comparable teaching labor.[26] With the increased potential for unionization of contingent faculty in public universities, the opportunity exists for support and advocacy from tenured faculty unions. At the University of Oregon, for example, a single contractual agreement covers both tenured and contingent faculty as well as library, emeritus, and research faculty under the umbrella of United Academics, American Association of University Professors/American Federation of Teachers, and the AFL-CIO.[27] The first agreement was reached with United Academics in 2013, just as the Oregon University System of seven public universities was being disbanded and separate governing boards were established for the University of Oregon and Portland State University.[28] The advantage of such an approach to a single contractual agreement is consolidated negotiations that address all faculty interests. One of the union's proposals for the delayed contract negotiations due to COVID-19 in 2021 was the creation of a "teaching professor" category that would grant tenure to career instructors following review of their pedagogy and curriculum.[29]

Another avenue for building solidarity among tenured and nontenured ranks is to capitalize on opportunities for these cohorts to integrate their work, whether within a department or across the university. For example, in professional development and orientation seminars as well as on university committees, the participation of both tenured and contingent faculty can offer opportunity for information sharing and building bridges.[30]

CONCLUSION

In a highly developed democratic nation such as the United States, the designation of an academic underclass for the teaching of many undergraduates represents a massive failure to invest in the educational process. On a personal level, we have seen the struggles of many contingent faculty to simply stay afloat financially while at the same time modeling values of critical thinking and academic excellence in the classroom. Many students may be unaware of the low pay that contingent faculty receive and the myriad challenges they face.

A stunning report titled "An Army of Temps" (2020) by the American Federation of Teachers found the following in a survey of 3,076 contingent faculty respondents in both two- and four-year institutions:

- One-third of the respondents earn less than $25,000 and fall below the poverty line for a family of four.
- Another third earn below $50,000 annually.
- Less than half have access to health insurance from their employer.
- Forty-one percent struggle with job insecurity, placing them below the federal poverty guideline for a family of four.
- Only 15 percent report that they can cover monthly expenses without difficulty.

Although most have been teaching more than ten years, 71.8 percent of respondents only have a contract for an academic term, leaving them in a state of constant anxiety about renewal. [31]

For minoritized contingent faculty, the double marginalization we have described throughout the book has left them in a particularly vulnerable position due to academic politics, budgetary cutbacks, and the recent tide of restrictive state legislation around diversity. Our study has particularly highlighted the intensification of exclusion resulting from the intersectionality of minoritized identities whether of race/ethnicity, gender, sexual orientation, gender identity, age, or disability. The poignant and searing narratives of our interviewees paint a picture of frequent stress around nonrenewal and issues that can arise from the escalation of student complaints about grades and student evaluations. Despite these many obstacles, our interviewees express their continued devotion to students and the educational process. But we cannot rely on the dedication and goodwill of contingent faculty indefinitely. Measures need to be taken to improve the potential for the establishment of career ladders with equitable pay and the potential for continuing appointment. The recent landmark contractual agreement at the University of California with contingent faculty is a major step in the right direction.

Contingent faculty, whether part-time or full-time, are an untapped and undervalued talent resource in higher education. The poet Jennifer Jean, a former adjunct, writes of the "adjunct shuffle" and the failure of institutions of higher education "to grow their own" and provide a pipeline for minoritized adjuncts to attain tenure-track positions. The lack of opportunity for career growth, the absence of benefits and competitive pay, and the failure to include contingent faculty in the larger community leaves some with little reason to invest in their institutions, regardless of the commitment to students in their classes. As Jean herself explains,

> When I was adjuncting, I'm sorry to say it, but I gave into despair. I absolutely love to teach—but I've taught at eight different universities and came to see them as interchangeable—just as they saw each body in "the adjunct pool" as interchangeable. As far as academia goes, it may be too late for me. But not for others—not for those just coming up in the world.[32]

It is still not too late to reconfigure contingent faculty working conditions, build more inclusive environments for minoritized contingent faculty, and ensure that employment equity is a grounding principle in higher education. If higher education is to serve as a bulwark of American democracy, it cannot ignore the inequitable treatment of a major segment of its faculty. To do so would be to undercut fundamental educational purposes in terms of student learning outcomes, research excellence, and service to the larger community. Tiffany Kraft, an activist and longtime adjunct, sums up the perils of the stigma of contingent faculty status:

I am stuck in a spiraling cycle, afraid to lose what little seniority I have as an affiliate adjunct, and I am stretched thin juggling heavy course loads, which makes it hard to look for work elsewhere or dig my way out this hole through publishing. . . . This stigma needs to change.

I can't say I've ever met a complacent adjunct, but I have met several who, like me, have both front and back burners on high. Sometimes I wonder how long I can sustain the workload without burning out or boiling over. Even after a decade of extreme adjuncting, what I find most oppressive is not the workload itself, but the cyclical fear of unemployment without benefits.[33]

Going forward, the imminent challenge to university and college administrations even in difficult budgetary times is to foreground student learning outcomes and fundamentally restructure contingent faculty practices in order to model and institutionalize organizational justice undergirded by the values of equity, diversity, and inclusion.

APPENDIX
Profile of Survey Respondents

OF THE TWENTY INTERVIEWEES, EIGHTEEN ARE CURRENTLY EMPLOYED AS contingent faculty members, while one former contingent faculty member is now a full-time tenured faculty member. Six currently hold adjunct appointments, and all but three contingent faculty work in doctoral research universities. Two respondents serve or have served as diversity officers, with one now holding a lecturer appointment. Fifteen of the individuals interviewed hold a PhD, and the remaining five hold master's degrees as the terminal degree. All but three of the respondents chose to remain anonymous and use pseudonyms.

The survey sample included individuals in all geographic areas including seven in the East, six in the Midwest, five in the West, one in the South, and one in the Southwest. The racial/ethnic representation of the interviewees is five white, two Latinx, seven Black, five Asian or Asian American, and one biracial. There were six male respondents, thirteen females, and one transgender female.

Table A.1 that follows lists presents the profiles of our survey respondents. Due to the need to protect confidentiality, we only provide general information about each respondent.

TABLE A.1 Profiles of interviewees

PSEUDONYM/ NAME	EMPLOYMENT STATUS	RACE/ ETHNICITY	GENDER	GENDER IDENTITY	DISABILITY	DEGREE	INSTITUTIONAL TYPE
Amy	Full-time contingent	White	Female			PhD	Doctoral research
Andrea	Adjunct	White	Female			MA	Doctoral research
David	Full-time contingent	Latino	Male			PhD	Doctoral research
Diane	Full-time contingent	Asian	Female			PhD	Doctoral research
Janice	Adjunct	Black	Female			PhD	Master's university
Julie	Full-time contingent	Biracial	Female			PhD	Doctoral research
Justin	Clinical professor	Black	Male			PhD	Doctoral research
LeeAnn	Administrator/adjunct	Black	Female			MA	Doctoral research
Margot	Adjunct	White	Female			PhD	Doctoral research
Marla	Former chief diversity officer/lecturer	Latina	Female			PhD	Doctoral research
Michael	Full-time contingent	Asian	Male			AbD	Doctoral research
Monica	Full-time contingent	Black	Female			PhD	Doctoral research
Wende Marshall	Adjunct	Black	Female		Disabled	PhD	Temple University
Robert Sellers	Chief diversity officer/ professor	Black	Male			PhD	University of Michigan

	Professor/former contingent faculty	Race	Gender				
Mark Purcell		White	Male			PhD	University of Washington
Nora	Full-time contingent	White	Female	Trans	Disabled	PhD	Doctoral research
Sahil	Full-time contingent	Asian	Male			MA	Doctoral research
Sara	Full-time contingent	Asian	Female			PhD	Doctoral research
Valerie	Full-time contingent	Black	Female			MA	Master's university
Viviana	Adjunct	Southeast Asian	Female			MBA	Doctoral research

NOTES

INTRODUCTION

1. Organization of American Historians, "In Memoriam: Thea K. Hunter," April 25, 2019, https://www.oah.org/insights/archive/in-memoriam-thea -k-hunter/.
2. Thea Hunter's story is documented in a poignant article by Adam Harris in *The Atlantic*. See A. Harris, "The Death of an Adjunct," *The Atlantic*, April 8, 2019, https://www.theatlantic.com/education/archive/2019/04/adjunct -professors-higher-education-thea-hunter/586168/.
3. Harris, "The Death of an Adjunct."
4. A. W. June, "Job Cuts and Stagnant Salaries: A New Report Details the Pandemic's Toll on the Faculty," *Chronicle of Higher Education*, March 20, 2021, https://www.chronicle.com/blogs/live-coronavirus-updates/job -cuts-and-stagnant-salaries-a-new-report-details-the-pandemics-toll-on -the-faculty.
5. D. Bauman, "Brutal Tally: Higher Ed Lost 650,000 Jobs Last Year," *Chronicle of Higher Education*, February 5, 2021, https://www.chronicle.com/article /a-brutal-tally-higher-ed-lost-650-000-jobs-last-year. See also D. Douglas-Gabriel and A. Fowers, "The Lowest Paid Workers in Higher Education Are Suffering the Highest Job Losses," *Washington Post*, November 17, 2020, https://www.washingtonpost.com/education/2020/11/17/higher -ed-job-loss/.
6. D. Bauman, "Here's Who Was Hardest Hit by Higher Ed's Pandemic-Driven Job Losses," *Chronicle of Higher Education*, April 19, 2021, https:// www.chronicle.com/article/heres-who-was-hit-hardest-by-higher-eds -pandemic-driven-job-losses.
7. K. W. Kim, A. Kalev, F. Dobbin, and G. Deutsch, "Crisis and Uncertainty: Did the Great Recession Reduce the Diversity of New Faculty?," *Sociological Science* 8 (2020): 308–24.
8. C. Chang, "How the Pandemic Has Pushed Contingent Faculty to the Precipice," *The Best Schools*, June 5, 2020, accessed April 4, 2021, https://the-bestschools.org/magazine/adjunct-layoffs-due-to-covid-19/.

9. D. Bauman, "After a Year of Losses, Higher Ed's Workforce Is Growing Again," *Chronicle of Higher Education*, July 8, 2021, https://www.chronicle .com/article/after-a-year-of-losses-higher-eds-work-force-is-growing-again.

10. E. Whitford, "Colleges Could Lose $183 Billion during Pandemic," Inside Higher Ed, February 8, 2021, https://www.insidehighered.com/quicktakes /2021/02/09/colleges-could-lose-183-billion-during-pandemic.

11. State Higher Education Executive Officers Association, *SHEF FY 2020*, 2021, https://shef.sheeo.org/wp-content/uploads/2021/05/SHEEO_SHEF _FY20_Report.pdf.

12. B. Quilantan, "Biden's Covid Relief Won't Shield Many Public Colleges from Pandemic's Blow," Politico, March 11, 2021, https://www.politico.com /news/2021/03/11/public-colleges-and-universities-brace-for-steep-budget -cuts-spurred-by-the-pandemic-475393.

13. B. Lovelli, "University Officials Push Back against Proposed Budget Cuts," Honolulu Civil Beat, May 2, 2021, https://www.civilbeat.org/2021/05 /university-of-hawaii-officials-push-back-against-proposed-budget-cuts/.

14. M. J. Finkelstein, V. M. Conley, and J. H. Schuster, "Taking the Measure of Faculty Diversity," TIAA-CREF Institute, April 2016, https://www .tiaa.org/content/dam/tiaa/institute/pdf/full-report/2017-02/taking-the -measure-of-faculty-diversity.pdf.

15. A. Kezar, T. DePaola, and D. T. Scott, *The Gig Academy: Mapping Labor in the Neoliberal University* (Baltimore: Johns Hopkins University Press, 2019), 15.

16. S. Slaughter and G. Rhoades, "The Neo-liberal University." *New Labor Forum* 6 (2009): 73–79.

17. Kezar, DePaola, and Scott, *The Gig Academy*, 16 (emphasis added).

18. National Center for Education Statistics, "Table 324.20. Doctor's Degrees Conferred by Postsecondary Institutions, by Race/Ethnicity and Sex of Student: Selected Years, 1976–77 through 2014–15," *Digest of Education Statistics*, accessed April 25, 2021, https://nces.ed.gov/programs/digest/d16/ tables/dt16_324.20.asp. See also National Center for Education Statistics, "The Condition of Education 2020," accessed April 25, 2021, https://nces .ed.gov/programs/coe/summary.asp.

19. H. Reichman, "Do Adjuncts Have Academic Freedom? Or Why Tenure Matters: The Costs of Contingency," *Academe* (Winter 2021), https://www .aaup.org/article/do-adjuncts-have-academic-freedom-or-why-tenure -matters#.YdxAFP7MI2w.

20. See, for example, American Federation of Teachers, "New Jersey Adjunct

Fired after Speaking Out," June 28, 2017, https://www.aft.org/news/new-jersey-adjunct-fired-after-speaking-out.

21. A. Kezar, D. Maxey, and L. Badke, "The Imperative for Change: Fostering Understanding of the Necessity of Changing Non-Tenure-Track Faculty Policies and Practices," The Delphi Project on the Changing Faculty and Student Success, 2014, https://pullias.usc.edu/download/imperative-change-fostering-understanding-necessity-changing-non-tenure-track-faculty-policies-practices/.

22. Kezar, DePaola, and Scott, *The Gig Academy.*

23. M. Purcell, "'Skilled, Cheap, and Desperate': Non-Tenure-Track Faculty and the Delusion of Meritocracy," *Antipode* (2007), 127.

24. Purcell, "'Skilled, Cheap, and Desperate,'" 121–22.

25. K. Tolley and E. Edwards, "Conclusion: Reflections on the Possibilities and Limitations of Collective Bargaining," in *Professors in the Gig Economy: Unionizing Adjunct Faculty in America,* ed. K. Tolley (Baltimore: Johns Hopkins University Press), 187.

26. J. Pfeffer, *Dying for a Paycheck: How Modern Management Harms Employee Health and Company Performance—and What We Can Do about It* (New York: HarperCollins, 2018). See also J. Goh, J. Pfeffer, and S. Zenios, "The Relationship between Workplace Stressors and Mortality and Health Costs in the United States," *Management Science* 62 (2016): 608–28.

27. G. Berryman, "The Secret Lives of Adjunct Professors," *Elle,* December 15, 2021, https://www.elle.com/life-love/a38424968/the-secret-lives-of-adjunct-professors/.

28. J. Bichsel, M. Fuesting, S. Nadel-Hawthorne, and A. Schmidt, "Faculty in Higher Education Annual Report: Key Findings, Trends, and Comprehensive Tables for Tenure-Track, Non-Tenure Teaching, and Non-Tenure Research Faculty and Summary Data for Adjunct Faculty for the 2020–21 Academic Year," CUPA-HR, March 2021, https://www.cupahr.org/wp-content/uploads/surveys/Results/2021_Faculty_Annual_Report_Overview.pdf./

29. American Association of University Professors, "The Annual Report on the Economic Status of the Profession, 2020–2021," July 2021, https://www.aaup.org/file/AAUP_ARES_2020-21.pdf.

30. L. Krantz, "In Higher Education, the Pandemic Has Been Especially Cruel to Adjunct Professors," *Boston Globe,* September 20, 2022, https://www.bostonglobe.com/2020/09/20/metro/pandemic-deepens-great-divide-academia/.

31. Quotations in this book are mainly from in-person interviews, and any

exceptions are footnoted. For further explanation, please see the section "Methodology for the Study" in this chapter.

32. D. Tomaskovic-Dewey and D. Avent-Holt, *Relational Inequalities: An Organizational Approach* (Oxford: Oxford University Press, 2020).

33. J. R. Feagin, *Systemic Racism: A Theory of Oppression* (New York: Routledge, 2006).

34. Tomaskovic-Dewey and Avent-Holt, *Relational Inequalities*.

35. C. J. Porter, C. M. Moore, G. J. Boss, T. J. Davis, and D. A. Louis, "To Be Black Women and Contingent Faculty: Four Personal Scholarly Narratives," *Journal of Higher Education* 91, no. 5 (2020): 674–97.

36. T. C. Sato, "Ignored, Pacified, and Deflected: Racial Battle Fatigue for an Asian American Non–Tenure Track Professor," in *Racial Battle Fatigue in Faculty: Perspectives and Lessons from Higher Education,* ed. N. D. Hartlep and D. Ball, 84–98 (New York: Routledge, 2019).

37. S. D. Museus and K. A. Griffin, "Mapping the Margins in Higher Education: On the Promise of Intersectionality Frameworks in Research and Discourse," in *Using Mixed-Methods Approaches to Study Intersectionality in Higher Education*, ed. K. A. Griffin and S. D. Museus, 5–13 (San Francisco: Wiley, 2011). See also E. Chun and A. Evans, *Leveraging Multigenerational Workforce Strategies in Higher Education* (New York: Routledge, 2021).

38. F. A. Bonner II, "'Mascu'sectionality: Theorizing an Alternative Framework for Black Males," Diverse Education, January 19, 2019, https://www.diverse education.com/demographics/african-american/article/15103947/ mascusectionality-theorizing-an-alternative-framework-for-black-males.

39. P. H. Collins, *Intersectionality as Critical Social Theory* (Durham, NC: Duke University Press, 2019).

40. P. H. Collins, "Learning from the Outsider Within: The Sociological Significance of Black Feminist Thought," in *Women in Higher Education: A Feminist Perspective*, ed. J. S. Glazer-Raymo, E. M. Bensimon, and B. K. Townsend (Needham Heights, MA: Ginn, 1993), 50.

41. K. Crenshaw, "Demarginalizing the Intersection of Race and Sex: A Black Feminist Critique of Antidiscrimination Doctrine, Feminist Theory and Antiracist Politics," *University of Chicago Legal Forum* 1989, no. 1 (1989): Article 8, http://chicagounbound.uchicago.edu/uclf/vol1989/iss1/8.

42. A. M. Smith, M. B. Watkins, J. J. Ladge, and P. Carlton, "Interviews with 59 Black Female Executives Explore Intersectional Invisibility and Strategies to Overcome It," *Harvard Business Review,* May 10, 2018, https://

hbr.org/2018/05/interviews-with-59-black-female-executives-explore
-intersectional-invisibility-and-strategies-to-overcome-it.

43. McKinsey & Company. "Women in the Workplace 2021," https://www
.mckinsey.com/~/media/mckinsey/featured%20insights/diversity%20
and%20inclusion/women%20in%20the%20workplace%202021/women
-in-the-workplace-2021.pdf.

44. T. M. Cottom, "The New Old Labor Crisis," *Slate*, January 24, 2014, https://
slate.com/human-interest/2014/01/adjunct-crisis-in-higher-ed-an-all-too
-familiar-story-for-black-faculty.html.

45. S. Carlson, E. Hoover, B. McMurtie, E. Pettit, and M. Zahneis, "Forced Out:
The Faces of Higher Ed's Layoffs," *Chronicle of Higher Education,* April 21,
2021, https://www.chronicle.com/article/forced-out.

46. "UIC UF NTT Job Security Press Conference," YouTube, May 20, 2021,
https://www.youtube.com/watch?v=csWKZyFl5UM.

47. H. Malinowitz, "The Faces of Austerity," *The Ithacan*, February 18, 2021,
https://theithacan.org/news/the-faces-of-austerity-feb-18/.

48. A. Paul, "Adjuncts Face Dire Situation as CUNY Downsizes," PSC CUNY,
December 2020, https://www.psc-cuny.org/clarion/december-2020/
adjuncts-face-dire-situation-cuny-downsizes.

49. Carlson et al., "Forced Out."

50. Carlson et al., "Forced Out."

51. C. Leddy, "CUNY Leaders Pressed on Thousands of Faculty Layoffs,"
Gotham Gazette, November 13, 2020, https://www.gothamgazette.com/state
/9905-cuny-leaders-pressed-layoffs-adjuncts-professors-city-council.

52. Leddy, "CUNY Leaders Pressed."

53. M. Elsen-Rooney, "CUNY Board of Trustees Tables Vote on $3 Million
Proposal after Criticism," *New York Daily News,* April 12, 2021, https://
www.nydailynews.com/new-york/education/ny-cuny-mckinsey-reopening
-plan-20210412-mogeiwjko5dgpdql3l3d2rsvyi-story.html.

54. M. Valbrun, "Lives and Livelihoods," Inside Higher Ed, June 23, 2020,
https://www.insidehighered.com/news/2020/06/23/cuny-system-suffers
-more-coronavirus-deaths-any-other-higher-ed-system-us.

55. Coalition of Rutgers Unions, "Rutgers Unions Say 'the Clock Is Ticking' on
Another Chance to Stop Layoffs and Cuts," Insider NJ, February 24, 2021,
https://www.insidernj.com/press-release/rutgers-unions-say-clock-ticking
-another-chance-stop-layoffs-cuts/.

56. Reichman, "Do Adjuncts Have Academic Freedom?"

57. R. Goist, "Arbitrator Sides with University of Akron in Layoff of Nearly 100 Union Faculty," Cleveland.com, September 18, 2020, https://www.cleveland .com/education/2020/09/arbitrator-sides-with-university-of-akron-in -layoff-of-nearly-100-union-faculty.html.

58. J. Pignolet, "Lack of Trust and Fear of Long-Term Damages Loom after University of Akron Faculty Layoffs," *Akron Beacon Journal*, October 24, 2020, https://www.beaconjournal.com/story/news/2020/10/04 /faculty-trust-eroded-after-university-akron-layoffs-covid-19-higher education/5890230002/. See also Goist, "Arbitrator Sides with University of Akron."

59. A. Kezar and C. Sam, "Governance as a Catalyst for Policy Change: Creating a Contingent Faculty Friendly Academy," *Educational Policy* 28, no. 3 (2014): 425–62.

60. For a full analysis of this issue, see E. B. Chun and J. R. Feagin, *Who Killed Higher Education: Maintaining White Dominance in a Desegregating Era* (New York: Routledge, 2022). See also State Higher Education Executive Officers Association, "State Higher Education Finance: FY 2019," 2020, https://shef.sheeo.org/wp-content/uploads/2020/04/SHEEO_SHEF _FY19_Report.pdf.

61. M. Burawoy, "Reconstructing Social Theories." In *Ethnography Unbound: Power and Resistance in the Modern Metropolis,* ed. M. Burawoy et al. (Berkeley: University of California Press, 1991), 10.

62. M. Burawoy, "The Extended Case Method." In *Ethnography Unbound: Power and Resistance in the Modern Metropolis*, ed. M. Burawoy et al., 271–87 (Berkeley: University of California Press, 1991).

CHAPTER 1

1. See, for example, L. Busch, *Knowledge for Sale: The Neoliberal Takeover of Higher Education* (Cambridge, MA: MIT Press, 2017); and A. Samalavičius, ed., *Neoliberalism, Economism, and Higher Education* (Newcastle upon Tyne, UK: Cambridge Scholars Publishing, 2018). See also M. L. Darden, *Entrepreneuring the Future of Higher Education: Radical Transformation in Times of Profound Change* (Lanham, MD: Rowman & Littlefield, 2021).

2. C. Newfield, *The Great Mistake: How We Wrecked Public Universities and How We Can Fix Them* (Baltimore: Johns Hopkins University Press, 2016).

3. H. A. Giroux, *Neoliberalism's War on Higher Education* (Chicago: Haymarket Books, 2014).

4. R. Hohle, *Racism in the Neoliberal Era: A Meta History of Elite White Power* (New York: Routledge, 2018).

5. S. Slaughter and G. Rhoades, "The Neo-liberal University," *New Labor Forum* 6 (2000): 73–79.

6. E. B. Chun and J. R. Feagin, *Who Killed Higher Education? Maintaining White Dominance in a Desegregating Era* (New York: Routledge, 2022).

7. A. Campbell, "The Birth of Neoliberalism in the United States: A Reorganisation of Capitalism," in *Neoliberalism: A Critical Reader*, ed. A. Saad-Filho and D. Johnston, 187–98 (Ann Arbor, MI: Pluto, 2005).

8. D. Harvey, *A Brief History of Neoliberalism* (Oxford: Oxford University Press, 2007).

9. P. Starr, *Entrenchment: Wealth, Power, and the Constitution of Democratic Societies* (New Haven, CT: Yale University Press, 2019), 169.

10. Chun and Feagin, *Who Killed Higher Education?*

11. R. Hohle, *Race and the Origins of American Neoliberalism* (New York: Routledge, 2015).

12. Hohle, *Race and the Origins of American Neoliberalism*, 7.

13. G. Hall, *The Uberfication of the University* (Minneapolis: University of Minnesota Press, 2016).

14. M. Friedman, *Capitalism and Freedom*, 40th anniversary ed. (Chicago: University of Chicago Press, 2002), 100.

15. J. M. Gappa, A. E. Austin, and A. G. Trice, *Rethinking Faculty Work: Higher Education's Strategic Imperative* (San Francisco: Jossey-Bass, 2007). See also Chun and Feagin, *Who Killed Higher Education?*

16. K. J. Dougherty and R. S. Natow, "Analysing Neoliberalism in Theory and Practice: The Case of Performance-Based Funding for Higher Education," Working paper no. 44, Centre for Global Higher Education, London, March 2019. See also Chun and Feagin, *Who Killed Higher Education?*

17. D. Maxey and A. Kezar, "The Current Context for Faculty Work in Higher Education," in *Envisioning Faculty Work for the Twenty-First Century: Moving to a Mission-Oriented and Learner-Centered Model*, ed. A. Kezar and D. Maxey, 3–22 (New Brunswick, NJ: Rutgers University Press, 2016).

18. Chun and Feagin, *Who Killed Higher Education?*

19. M. Huelsman, "Social Exclusion: The State of State U for Black Student," Demos, 2018, www.demos.org/research/social-exclusion-state-state-u-black-students.

20. L. Davis and R. Fry, "College Faculty Have Become More Racially and

Ethnically Diverse, but Remain Far Less So Than Students," Fact Tank, Pew Research Center, July 31, 2019, https://www.pewresearch.org/fact-tank /2019/07/31/us-college-faculty-student-diversity/.

21. H. Childress, *The Adjunct Underclass: How America's Colleges Betrayed Their Faculty, Their Students, and Their Mission* (Chicago: University of Chicago Press, 2019).

22. Childress, *The Adjunct Underclass.*

23. B. J. Taylor, B. Cantwell, K. Watts, and O. Wood. "Partisanship, White Racial Resentment, and State Support for Higher Education," *Journal of Higher Education* 91, no. 6, (2020): 858–87. See also B. J. Taylor and B. Cantwell, *Unequal Higher Education: Wealth, Status, and Student Opportunity* (New Brunswick, NJ: Rutgers University Press), 2019.

24. M. K. McClendon, J. C. Hearn, and C. J. Mokher, "Partisans, Professionals, and Power: The Role of Political Factors in State Higher Education Funding," *Journal of Higher Education* 80, no. 6 (2009): 686–713.

25. State Higher Education Executive Officers Association, "State Higher Education Finance: FY 2019." 2020, https://shef.sheeo.org/wp-content /uploads/2020/04/SHEEO_SHEF_FY19_Report.pdf.

26. R. Brownstein, "American Higher Education Hits a Dangerous Milestone," *The Atlantic,* May 3, 2018, https://www.theatlantic.com/politics/archive /2018/05/american-higher-education-hits-a-dangerous-milestone/559457/.

27. T. G. Mortenson, "State Funding: A Race to the Bottom," American Council on Education, 2012, https://www.acesconnection.com/g/aces-in-education /blog/state-funding-a-race-to-the-bottom-american-council-on-education.

28. V. Jackson and M. Saenz, "States Can Choose Better Path for Higher Education Funding in Covid-19 Recession," Center on Budget and Policy Priorities, February 17, 2021, https://www.cbpp.org/research/state-budget-and-tax /states-can-choose-better-path-for-higher-education-funding-in-covid.

29. D. Allen and G. C. Wolniak, "Exploring the Effects of Tuition Increases on Racial/Ethnic Diversity at Public Colleges and Universities," *Research in Higher Education* 60 (2019): 18–43.

30. State Higher Education Executive Officers Association, "State Higher Education Finance: FY 2019," 2020, https://shef.sheeo.org/wp-content /uploads/2020/04/SHEEO_SHEF_FY19_Report.pdf.

31. National Education Association, "Corona Virus Relief for Higher Education Toolkit," April 15, 2021, https://www.nea.org/resource-library/higher -education-covid-19-relief-briefing.

32. E. Whitford, "How Federal Stimulus Spending Plays Out for State Higher Education," Inside Higher Ed, May 28, 2021, https://www.insidehighered.com/news/2021/05/28/federal-stimulus-higher-ed-replay-2009.

33. S. Laderman and T. Harnisch, "Analysis of Federal Stimulus Funding to States and Public Institutions of Higher Education," State Higher Education Executive Officers Association, 2021, https://shef.sheeo.org/wp-content/uploads/2021/05/SHEEO_SHEF_FY20_IB_Federal_Stimulus.pdf.

34. M. J. Finkelstein, V. M. Conley, and J. H. Schuster, *The Faculty Factor: Reassessing the American Academy in Turbulence* (Baltimore: Johns Hopkins University Press, 2016). See also J. Del Gandio, "Neoliberalism, Higher Education, and the Rise of Contingent Faculty Labor," *Public Eye Magazine,* October 15, 2014, https://politicalresearch.org/2014/10/15/neoliberalism-higher-education-and-the-rise-of-contingent-faculty-labor.

35. Maxey and Kezar, "The Current Context for Faculty Work."

36. E. L. Boyer, *Scholarship Reconsidered: Priorities of the Professoriate* (Princeton, NJ: Carnegie Foundation for the Advancement of Teaching, 1990), 24.

37. S. Gehrke and A. Kezar, "Understanding the Faculty Role in Higher Education: Utilizing Historical, Theoretical, and Empirical Frameworks to Inform Future Research," in *Higher Education: Handbook of Theory and Research,* ed. M. B. Paulsen, 93–150 (Cham, Switzerland: Springer International, 2015).

38. A. Kezar, T. DePaola, and D. T. Scott, *The Gig Academy: Mapping Labor in the Neoliberal University* (Baltimore: Johns Hopkins University Press, 2019).

39. M. A. Chesler and A. A. Young Jr., eds., *Faculty Identities and the Challenges of Diversity: Reflections on Teaching in Higher Education* (Boulder, CO: Paradigm Publishers, 2013).

40. Gehrke and Kezar, "Understanding the Faculty Role in Higher Education."

41. X. Ran and D. Xu, "How and Why Do Adjunct Instructors Affect Students' Academic Outcomes? Evidence from Two-Year and Four-Year Colleges," CAPSEE working paper, Community College Research Center, Teachers College, Columbia University, 2017, https://academiccommons.columbia.edu/doi/10.7916/D80V8JDP.

42. S. Slaughter and G. Rhoades, *Academic Capitalism and the New Economy: Market, State, and Higher Education* (Baltimore: Johns Hopkins University Press, 2004).

43. Finkelstein, Conley, and Schuster, *The Faculty Factor.*

44. J. B. Powers, "Technology Transfer, Commercialization, and Proprietary

Science," in *The Business of Higher Education (2), Management and Fiscal Strategies*, ed. J. C. Knapp and D. J. Siegel, 73–95 (Santa Barbara, CA: ABC/CLIO-Praeger, 2009). See also A. Kezar, *How Colleges Change: Understanding, Leading, and Enacting Change* (New York: Routledge, 2014).

45. Slaughter and Rhoades, "The Neo-liberal University."

46. A. S. Metcalf and S. Slaughter, "The Differential Effects of Academic Capitalism on Women in the Academy," in *Unfinished Agendas: New and Continuing Gender Challenges in Higher Education*, ed. J. Glazer-Raymo, 80–111 (Baltimore: Johns Hopkins University Press, 2008).

47. E. Chun and A. Evans, *Leveraging Multigenerational Workforce Strategies in Higher Education* (New York: Routledge, 2021). Regarding the valorizing of research, see J. E. Cooper, A. M. Ortiz, M. K. P. Benham, and M. W. Scherr, "Finding a Home in the Academy: Confronting Racism and Ageism," in *Tenure in the Sacred Grove: Issues and Strategies for Women and Minority Faculty*, ed. J. E. Cooper and D. D. Stevens, 71–88 (Albany: State University of New York Press, 2002).

48. For a full discussion of Koch-supported think tanks and other conservative foundations, see Chun and Feagin, *Who Killed Higher Education?*

49. Mercatus Center, "About," George Mason University, accessed June 22, 2020, www.mercatus.org/about#:~:text=Our%20mission%20is%20to%20generate,%2C%20prosperous%2C%20and%20peaceful%20lives.

50. B. Mintz, "Neoliberalism and the Crisis in Higher Education: The Cost of Ideology," *American Journal of Economics and Sociology* 80, no. 1 (2021): 79–112.

51. R. J. Kreitzer and J. Sweet-Cushman, "Evaluating Student Evaluations of Teaching: A Review of Measurement and Equity Bias in SETs and Recommendations for Ethical Reform," *Journal of Academic Ethics* 20, no. 1 (2021): 73–84. See also C. Flaherty, "The Skinny on Teaching Evals and Bias," Inside Higher Ed, February 17, 2021, https://www.insidehighered.com/news/2021/02/17/whats-really-going-respect-bias-and-teaching-evals.

52. Kezar, DePaola, and Scott, *The Gig Academy*.

53. A. Calma and C. Dickson-Deane, "The Student as Customer and Quality in Higher Education," *International Journal of Educational Management* 34, no. 8 (2020): 1221–35.

54. American Council on Education, "Comprehensive Demographic Profile of American College Presidents Shows Slow Progress in Diversifying Leadership Ranks, Concerns about Funding," June 20, 2017, https://www.acenet.edu/News-Room/Pages/Comprehensive-Demographic-Profile-of

-American-College-Presidents-Shows-Slow-Progress-in-Diversifying
-Leadership-Ranks.aspx.

55. National Association of College and University Business Officers, "National Profile of Higher Education Business Officers Released," August 9, 2021, https://www.nacubo.org/Press-Releases/2021/National-Profile-of -Higher-Education-Chief-Business-Officers-Released.

56. R. Koenig, "'Academic Capitalism' Is Reshaping Faculty Life. What Does That Mean?," EdSurge, November 25, 2019, https://www.edsurge.com /news/2019-11-25-academic-capitalism-is-reshaping-faculty-life-what -does-that-mean.

57. H. Reichman, "Do Adjuncts Have Academic Freedom?," American Association of University Professors, Winter 2021, https://www.aaup.org/article /do-adjuncts-have-academic-freedom-or-why-tenure-matters.

58. National Association of College and University Business Officers, "2021 National Profile of Higher Education Chief Business Officers," 2021, https://www.nacubo.org/-/media/Documents/Research/2021-National -Profile-of-Higher-Education-Chief-Business-OfficersRevised1221.ash.

59. K. Robertson, "Nikole Hannah-Jones Denied Tenure at University of North Carolina," New York Times, May 19, 2021, https://www.nytimes .com/2021/05/19/business/media/nikole-hannah-jones-unc.html?referring Source=articleShare.

60. B. McConnell, "'A Blatant Disregard' UNC Journalism Faculty Criticize Trustees for Hannah-Jones Controversy," Chapelboro.com, June 4, 2021, https://chapelboro.com/news/unc/a-blatant-disregard-unc-journalism -faculty-criticize-trustees-for-hannah-jones-controversy.

61. C. Flaherty, "'A Blatant Intrusion,'" Inside Higher Ed, May 20, 2021, https:// www.insidehighered.com/news/2021/05/20/unc-chapel-hill-board-doesnt -approve-tenure-noted-journalist.

62. Y. Dzhanova, "The Creator of the 1619 Project Is Considering Bringing a Discrimination Lawsuit against UNC after She Was Denied Tenure," Business Insider, May 29, 2021, https://www.nytimes.com/2021/05/19/business /media/nikole-hannah-jones-unc.html?referringSource=articleShare.

63. K. Robertson, "Nikole Hannah-Jones Is Granted Tenure after Weekslong Dispute," New York Times, June 30, 2021, https://www.nytimes.com/2021 /06/30/business/media/nikole-hannah-jones-unc-tenure.html?referring Source=articleShare.

64. J. Dhillon, C. Arruzza, and AAUP-TNS Media Collective, "Corporate

Consultants Set Their Targets on American Universities," *The Nation*, October 23, 2020, https://www.thenation.com/article/society/new-school-huron/.

65. See also A. Bardia, S. Yadav, R. Kalpa, and A. Sg, "The New School Is in Crisis," *Jacobin Magazine,* December 2020, https://jacobinmag.com/2020/12/the-new-school-nssr-austerity-covid-neoliberalism.

66. Bardia et al., "The New School Is in Crisis."

67. American Association of University Professors, "New School Imposes Austerity, Slashes Vital and Vulnerable Staff," October 5, 2020, https://www.thenewschoolaaup.org/actions/oct05-press-statement.

68. G. Bellafante, "This School Was Built for Idealists. It Could Use Some Rich Alumni," *New York Times,* October 18, 2020, https://www.nytimes.com/2020/10/16/nyregion/new-school-nyc-endowment-layoffs.html?referringSource=articleShare.

69. Dhillon et al., "Corporate Consultants Set Their Targets."

70. Bardia et al., "The New School Is in Crisis."

71. Dhillon et al., "Corporate Consultants Set Their Targets."

72. University of New Hampshire, "Update No. 17 from President Dean," January 17, 2020, https://www.unh.edu/main/update-no-17-president-dean.

73. Huron, "University of New Hampshire Executive Summary: Resource Assessment and Academic Program Cost," March 3, 2020, https://www.unh.edu/sites/default/files/unh_plc_huron_findings_final_updated_3.3.20.pdf.

74. C. Flaherty, "Prioritization Anxiety," Inside Higher Ed, August 16, 2016. https://www.insidehighered.com/news/2016/08/16/how-can-increasingly-popular-academic-review-process-seem-more-meaningful-faculty.

75. M. J. Bresciani Lukvik, *Outcomes-Based Program Review: Closing Achievement Gaps In- and Outside the Classroom with Alignment to Predictive Analytics and Performance Metrics,* 2nd ed. (Sterling, VA: Stylus Publishing, 2018), 19. For references to the higher education industry, see, for example, 22, 49, and 82.

76. Flaherty, "Prioritization Anxiety."

CHAPTER 2

1. See L. A. Bolitzer, "What We Know (and Don't Know) about Adjunct Faculty at Four Year Institutions," *Review of Higher Education* 43, no. 1 (2019): 113–42. Our analysis of the demographics of both full- and part-time contingent faculty in four-year institutions includes the Carnegie classification of baccalaureate/associate colleges with four-year degrees.

2. Bolitzer, "What We Know." See also J. Naughton, H. A. Garcia, and K. Nehls, "Understanding the Growth of Contingent Faculty," in *Hidden and Visible: The Role and Impact of Contingency Faculty in Higher Education,* ed. J. Naughton, H. A. Garcia, and K. Nehls, 9–26 (Hoboken, NJ: Wiley).

3. Naughton, Garcia, and Nehls, "Understanding the Growth of Contingent Faculty."

4. The Delphi Project, "National Trends for Faculty Composition over Time," Pullias Center for Higher Education, University of Southern California, 2013, https://pullias.usc.edu/download/national-trends-faculty-composition -time/. See also D. Maxey and A. Kezar, "Revealing Opportunities and Obstacles for Changing Non-Tenure-Track Faculty Practices: An Examination of Stakeholders' Awareness of Institutional Contradictions," *Journal of Higher Education* 86, no. 4 (2015): 564–94.

5. M. J. Finkelstein, V. Conley, and J. H. Schuster, *The Faculty Factor: Reassessing the American Academy in a Turbulent Era* (Baltimore: Johns Hopkins University Press, 2016), table 3.5, 74–77. Note: Sources for the data are listed as IPEDS:93, IPEDS:03, and IPEDS:13. There is slight variation in the data when compared the Department of Education's *Digest of Education Statistics* shown in table 2.1 that is likely attributed to the filters used by these researchers.

6. P. W. Magness, "For-Profit Universities and the Roots of Adjunctification in US Higher Education," *Liberal Education* (Spring 2016): 50–59.

7. J. Brennan and P. W. Magness, "Are Adjunct Faculty Exploited? Some Grounds for Skepticism," *Journal of Business Ethics* 152 (2016): 54.

8. US Department of Education, National Center for Education Statistics, "Integrated Postsecondary Education Data System," Spring 2000 through Spring 2019, Human Resources component, Fall Staff section, https://nces .ed.gov/ipeds/.

9. Finkelstein, Conley and Schuster, *The Faculty Factor*, 14.

10. Brennan and Magness, "Are Adjunct Faculty Exploited?"

11. US Department of Education, *Digest of Education Statistics, 2014*, table 315.50, 2014, https://nces.ed.gov/pubs2016/2016006.pdf.

12. Brennan and Magness, "Are Adjunct Faculty Exploited?," 56.

13. M. Purcell, "'Skilled, Cheap, and Desperate': Non-Tenure-Track Faculty and the Delusion of Meritocracy," *Antipode*, 127.

14. Purcell, "'Skilled, Cheap, and Desperate.'"

15. M. J. Finkelstein, V. M. Conley, and J. J. Schuster, "Taking the Measure

of Faculty Diversity," TIAA-CREF Institute, April 2016, https://www
.tiaa.org/content/dam/tiaa/institute/pdf/full-report/2017-02/taking-the
-measure-of-faculty-diversity.pdf.

16. US Department of Education, National Center for Education Statistics,
"Integrated Postsecondary Education Data System," Spring 2019.

17. P. Yakoboski, "Adjunct Faculty: Who They Are and What Is Their Experience?," TIAA Institute, November 2018, https://www.tiaa.org/public
/institute/publication/2018/adjunct-faculty-survey-2018.

18. A. B. Fulk, "Confronting Biases against Adjunct Faculty," Inside Higher
Ed, February 14, 2019, https://www.insidehighered.com/advice/2019/02/14
/how-bias-toward-adjuncts-plays-out-among-students-other-faculty-and
-administrators.

CHAPTER 3

1. J. M. Gappa, "The Stress-Producing Working Conditions of Part-Time
Faculty," in *Coping with Faculty Stress*, ed. P. Seldin, 33–42 (San Francisco:
Jossey-Bass, 1987).

2. See J. Brennan and P. W. Magness, "Are Adjunct Faculty Exploited? Some
Grounds for Skepticism," *Journal of Business Ethics* 152 (2016): 54.

3. See, for example, T. F. Pettigrew, and J. Martin, "Shaping the Organizational
Context for Black American Inclusion," *Journal of Social Issues* 43, no. 1 (1987):
41–78; A. Evans and E. B. Chun, *Are the Walls Really Down? Behavioral
and Organizational Barriers to Faculty and Staff Diversity* (San Francisco:
Jossey-Bass, 2007); and E. B. Chun and J. R. Feagin, *Rethinking Diversity
Frameworks in Higher Education* (New York: Routledge, 2020).

4. See, for example, T. D. Joseph and L. Hirshfield, "'Why don't you get somebody new to do it?': Race, Gender, and Identity Taxation," in *Faculty Social
Identity and the Challenges of Diverse Classrooms in a Historically White University*, ed. M. Chesler and A. A. Young Jr., 153–69 (Boulder, CO: Paradigm
Publishers, 2013).

5. E. B. Stolzenberg et al., "Undergraduate Teaching Faculty: The Heri Faculty
Survey 2016–2017," Higher Education Research Institute at UCLA, 2017,
https://heri.ucla.edu/monographs/HERI-FAC2017-monograph.pdf.

6. W. A. Smith, M. Hung, and J. D. Franklin, "Racial Battle Fatigue and the
Miseducation of Black Men: Racial Microaggressions, Societal Problems,
and Environmental Stress," *Journal of Negro Education* 80, no. 1 (2011): 63–82.

7. M. A. Chesler, "The State of Research with Faculty Identities in Higher
Educational Classrooms and Institutional Contexts," in *Faculty Identities*

and the Challenge of Diversity: Reflections on Teaching in Higher Education, ed. M. A. Chesler and A. A. Young Jr., 1–20 (New York: Routledge, 2013).

8. A. Kezar, T. DePaola, and D. T. Scott, *The Gig Academy: Mapping Labor in the Neoliberal University* (Baltimore: Johns Hopkins University Press, 2019).

9. A. Bavishi, J. M. Madera, and M. R. Hebl, "The Effect of Professor Ethnicity and Gender on Student Evaluations: Judged before Met," *Journal of Diversity in Higher Education* 3, no. 4 (2010): 245–56. See also S. L. Wallace, A. K. Lewis, and M. Allen, "The State of the Literature on Student Evaluations of Teaching and an Exploratory Analysis of Written Comments: Who Benefits Most?," *College Teaching* 67, no. 1 (2019): 1–11.

10. R. J. Kreitzer and J. Sweet-Cushman, "Evaluating Student Evaluations of Teaching: A Review of Measurement and Equity Bias in SETs and Recommendations for Ethical Reform," *Journal of Academic Ethics* (2021): 1–12; and C. Flaherty, "The Skinny on Teaching Evals and Bias," Inside Higher Ed, February 17, 2021, https://www.insidehighered.com/news/2021/02/17/whats -really-going-respect-bias-and-teaching-evals.

11. H-J. Tiede, "The 2021 AAUP Shared Governance Survey: Findings on Demographics of Senate Chairs and Governance Structures," *Academe*, 2021, https://www.aaup.org/article/2021-aaup-shared-governance-survey -findings-demographics-senate-chairs-and-governance#.YW2GwxrMI2w.

12. H-J. Tiede, "The 2021 AAUP Shared Governance Survey."

13. American Association of University Professors, "The Inclusion in Governance of Faculty Members Holding Contingent Appointments," 2012, https://www.aaup.org/report/inclusion-governance-faculty-members -holding-contingent-appointments.

14. J. T. Minor, "Faculty Diversity and the Traditions of Academic Governance," in *Measuring Glass Ceiling Effects in Higher Education: Opportunities and Challenges*, ed. J. F. L. Jackson, E. M. O'Callaghan, and R. A. Leon, 49–61 (San Francisco: Jossey-Bass, 2014).

15. For further discussion of the role of contingent faculty in change processes, see A. Kezar and C. Sam, "Governance as a Catalyst for Policy Change: Creating a Contingent Faculty Friendly academy," *Educational Policy* 28, no. 3 (2014): 425–62.

CHAPTER 4

1. E. Chun and A. Evans, *Leading a Diversity Culture Shift in Higher Education: Comprehensive Organizational Learning Strategies* (New York: Routledge, 2018).

2. V. J. Roscigno, S. H. Lopez, and R. Hodson, "Supervisory Bullying, Status Inequalities and Organizational Context," *Social Forces* 87, no. (2009): 1561–89.

3. K. Edwards and K. Tolley, "Do Unions Help Adjuncts?," *Chronicle of Higher Education,* June 3, 2018, https://www.chronicle.com/article/do-unions-help -adjuncts/. For the list of institutions, see K. Tolley, ed., *Professors in the Gig Economy: Unionizing Adjunct Faculty in America* (Baltimore: Johns Hopkins University Press, 2018), 187–202.

4. N. D. Hartlep and D. Ball, "The Battle of Racial Battle Fatigue," in *Racial Battle Fatigue in Faculty: Perspectives and Lessons from Higher Education,* ed. N. D. Hartlep and D. Ball, 1–13 (New York: Routledge, 2020).

5. See University of California, Office of the President, "Academic Personnel and Programs, accessed August 18, 2021, https://www.ucop.edu/academic -personnel-programs/academic-personnel-policy/appointment-and -promotion/index.html.

6. S. K. Kang, "Beyond the Double-Jeopardy Hypothesis: Examining the Interaction between Age- and Race-Based Stereotypes across the Lifespan" (PhD dissertation, University of Toronto, 2010).

7. See E. Chun and A. Evans, *Leveraging Multigenerational Workforce Strategies in Higher Education* (New York: Routledge, 2021).

8. R. F. Gregory, *Age Discrimination in the American Workplace: Old at a Young Age* (Piscataway, NJ: Rutgers University Press, 2001). For further discussion, see Chun and Evans, *Leveraging Multigenerational Workforce Strategies.*

9. V. J. Roscigno, "Ageism in the American Workforce," *Contexts*, no. 9 (2010): 16–21.

10. M. A. Chesler, "The State of Research with Faculty Identities in Higher Educational Classrooms and Institutional Contexts," in *Faculty Identities and the Challenge of Diversity: Reflections on Teaching in Higher Education,* ed. M. A. Chesler and A. A. Young Jr., 1–20 (New York: Routledge, 2013).

11. J. Crocker, K. Vole, M. Test, and B. Major, "Social Stigma: The Affective Consequences of Attributional Ambiguity," *Journal of Personality and Social Psychology* 60, no. 2 (1991): 218–28.

12. J. W. Kunstman, T. Tuscherer, S. Trawalter, and E. P. Lloyd, "What Lies Beneath? Minority Group Members' Suspicion of Whites' Egalitarian Motivation Predicts Responses to Whites' Smiles," *Personality and Social Psychology Bulletin* 42, no. 9 (2016): 1193–205.

13. R. S. Lazarus, "Theory-Based Stress Management," *Psychological Inquiry* 1, no. 1 (1990): 3–13.

14. Crocker et al., "Social Stigma."

15. H. Ibarra, N. M. Carter, and C. Silva, "Why Men Still Get More Promotions Than Women," *Harvard Business Review* 88, no. 9 (September 2010): 80–126.

16. B. Ropers-Huilman, "Women Faculty and the Dance of Identities: Constructing Self and Privilege within Community," in *Unfinished Agendas: New and Continuing Gender Challenges in Higher Education*, ed. J. Glazer-Raymo, 35–51 (Baltimore: Johns Hopkins University Press, 2008).

CHAPTER 5

1. M. Purcell, "'Skilled, Cheap, and Desperate': Non-Tenure-Track Faculty and the Delusion of Meritocracy," *Antipode* (2007): 121–43.

2. J. R. Goez, "Exploring How an Academic Institution Implements a Diversity, Equity, and Inclusion Initiative in a Non-Tenure-Track Environment" (PhD dissertation, Teachers College, Columbia University, 2021), 99.

3. Goez, "Exploring How an Academic Institution Implements," 84.

4. Purcell, "'Skilled, Cheap, and Desperate,'" 126.

5. D. Maxey, and A. Kezar, "Revealing Opportunities and Obstacles for Changing Non-Tenure-Track Faculty Practices: An Examination of Stakeholders' Awareness of Institutional Contradictions," *Journal of Higher Education* 86, no. 4 (2015): 564–94.

6. J. M. Gappa and D. W. Leslie, *The Invisible Faculty: Improving the Status of Part-Timers in Higher Education* (San Francisco: Jossey-Bass, 1993).

7. S. Aryee, P. S. Budhwar, and Z. X. Chen, "Trust as a Mediator of the Relationship between Organizational Justice and Work Outcomes: Test of a Social Exchange Model," *Journal of Organizational Behavior* 23 (2002): 267–85.

8. A. A. Lebbaeus and O. Mensah, "To What Extent Does Employees' Perception of Organizational Justice Influence Their Organizational Citizenship Behaviour?," *European Journal of Business and Management* 5, no. 16 (2013): 32–41.

9. J. M. Gappa, A. E. Austin, and A. G. Trice, *Rethinking Faculty Work: Higher Education's Strategic Imperative* (San Francisco: Jossey-Bass, 2007). See also E. B. Chun and J. R. Feagin, *Who Killed Higher Education? Maintaining White Dominance in a Desegregating Era* (New York: Routledge, 2022); and J. M. Gappa, A. E. Austin, and A. G. Trice, "Rethinking Academic Work and Workplaces," *Change* 37, no. 6 (2005): 32–39.

10. See E. Chun and A. Evans, *Bridging the Diversity Divide: Globalization and Reciprocal Empowerment in Higher Education,* ASHE Higher Education Report 35, no. 1 (San Francisco: Jossey-Bass, 2009). The principle of reciprocal empowerment is defined by I. Prilleltensky, and L. Gonick, "The Discourse of Oppression in the Social Sciences: Past, Present, and Future," in *Human Diversity: Perspectives on People in Context, in* E. J. Trickett, R. J. Watts, and D. Birman, 145–77 (San Francisco: Jossey-Bass, 1994).

11. See T. C. Sato, "Ignored, Pacified, and Deflected: Racial Battle Fatigue for an Asian American Non–Tenure Track Professor," in *Racial Battle Fatigue in Faculty: Perspectives and Lessons from Higher Education,* ed. N. D. Hartlep and D. Ball, 84–98 (New York: Routledge, 2020).

12. A. Kezar, "Departmental Cultures and Non-Tenure-Track Faculty: Willingness, Capacity, and Opportunity to Perform at Four-Year Institutions," *Journal of Higher Education* 84, no. 2 (2013): 153–88.

13. E. Chun and J. R. Feagin, *Rethinking Diversity Frameworks in Higher Education* (New York: Routledge, 2021).

14. H. Fuchs, "Trump Attack on Diversity Training Has a Quick and Chilling Effect," *New York Times,* October 13, 2020, https://www.nytimes.com/2020/10/13/us/politics/trump-diversity-training-race.html?referringSource=articleShare.

15. D. J. Trump, "Executive Order on Combating Race and Sex Stereotyping," White House Archives, September 22, 2020, https://trumpwhitehouse.archives.gov/presidential-actions/executive-order-combating-race-sex-stereotyping/.

16. B. Wallace-Wells, "How a Conservative Activist Invented the Conflict over Critical Race Theory," *New Yorker,* June 18, 2021, https://www.newyorker.com/news/annals-of-inquiry/how-a-conservative-activist-invented-the-conflict-over-critical-race-theory.

17. C. Lang, "President Trump Has Attacked Critical Race Theory. Here's What to Know about the Intellectual Movement," *Time,* September 29, 2020, https://time.com/5891138/critical-race-theory-explained/.

18. D. Bell, "Epilogue: Affirmative Action: Another Instance of Racial Workings in the United States," *Journal of Negro Education* 69, nos. 1–2 (2000): 93–99.

19. See Z. Cheney-Rice, "The Right's New Reason to Panic about 'Critical Race Theory' Is Centuries Old," *New York Magazine,* June 30, 2021, https://nymag.com/intelligencer/2021/06/the-white-panic-behind-critical-race-theory.html. See also C. M. Blow, "White Racial Anxiety Strikes Again,"

New York Times, November 3, 2021, https://www.nytimes.com/2021/11/03 /opinion/youngkin-virginia-race.html.

20. S. Schwartz, "Map: Where Critical Race Theory Is under Attack," Education Week, June 13, 2023, https://www.edweek.org/policy-politics/map-where -critical-race-theory-is-under-attack/2021/06.

21. N. Austin-Hilary and V. Strang, "Racism's Prominent Role in January 6 US Capitol Attack," Human Rights Watch, January 5, 2022, https://www.hrw. org/news/2022/01/05/racisms-prominent-role-january-6-us-capitol-attack.

22. J. Leonard and N. Cook, "Biden Says 'White Supremacy' Drove Trump's January 6 Rioters," Bloomberg, October 21, 2021, https://www.bloomberg .com/news/articles/2021-10-21/biden-says-white-supremacy-motivated -trump-s-jan-6-rioters.

23. E. Pettit, "'It just felt wrong': U. of Florida Faculty Say Political Fears Stalled an Initiative on Race," *Chronicle of Higher Education,* November 30, 2021, https://www.chronicle.com/article/it-just-felt-wrong-u-of-florida -faculty-say-political-fears-stalled-an-initiative-on-race.

24. B. C. Calvan, "Florida Bans 'Critical Race Theory' from Its Classrooms," Associated Press, June 10, 2021, https://apnews.com/article/florida-race -and-ethnicity-government-and-politics-education-74d0af6c52c0009 ec3fa3ee9955b0a8d WTTW .

25. WXTL, "New Bill Would Ban Critical Race Theory from Florida Public Universities, State Colleges," September 15, 2021, https://www.wtxl.com /news/local-news/new-bill-would-ban-critical-race-theory-from-florida -public-universities-state-colleges.

26. T. Bella, "DeSantis Invokes MLK as He Proposes Stop Woke Act against Critical Race Theory," *Washington Post*, December 15, 2021, https://www .washingtonpost.com/politics/2021/12/15/desantis-stop-woke-act-mlk-crt/.

27. A. Nierenberg, "What Does 'Don't Say Gay' Actually Say?," *New York Times*, March 23, 2022, https://www.nytimes.com/2022/03/23/us/what-does-dont -say-gay-actually-say.html.

28. Petitt, "'It just felt wrong.'" See also Florida Senate, "HB 57: Racial and Sexual Discrimination," 2022, https://www.flsenate.gov/Session/Bill/2022/57.

29. Florida Senate, "CS/CS/CS/SB 266: Higher Education," 2023, https:// www.flsenate.gov/Session/Bill/2023/266.

30. Florida College System College of Presidents, "Florida College System Presidents Statement on Diversity, Equity, Inclusion and Critical Race Theory," January 18, 2023, https://www.fldoe.org/core/fileparse.php/5673/urlt

/FCSDEIstatement.pdf. See also B. Rosenberg, "The Deafening Silence of Florida's College Presidents," *Chronicle of Higher Education*, April 6, 2023, https://www.chronicle.com/article/the-deafening-silence-of-floridas -college-presidents.

31. American Association of University Professors, "Preliminary Report of the Special Committee on Academic Freedom and Florida," May 24, 2023, https://www.aaup.org/file/Preliminary_Report_Florida.pdf.

32. C. R. Hodges and O. M. Welch, "Making Noise and Good, Necessary Trouble: Dilemmas of 'Deaning While Black,'" in *Dismantling Institutional Whiteness: Emerging Forms of Leadership in Higher Education*, ed. M. C. Alcade and M. Subramaniam, 55–77 (West Lafayette, IN: Purdue University Press, 2023).

33. See, for example, Gappa, Austin, and Trice, "Rethinking Academic Work and Workplaces."

34. M. M. Crow, and W. B. Dabars, *Designing the New American University* (Baltimore: Johns Hopkins University Press, 2015).

35. J. Liu, "A Record 4.4 Million People Quit in September as Great Resignation Shows No Signs of Stopping," CNBC, November 12, 2021, https:// www.cnbc.com/2021/11/12/a-record-4point4-million-people-quit-jobs -in-september-great-resignation.html.

36. McKinsey & Company, "Winning with Your Talent Management Strategy," 2018, https://www.mckinsey.com/business-functions/people-and -organizational-performance/our-insights/winning-with-your-talent -management-strategy. See also E. Chun and A. Evans, "Designing and Implementing Strategies for the Development of a Winning Faculty Workforce," TIAA Institute, 2014, https://www.tiaainstitute.org/sites /default/files/presentations/2017-02/designing-and-implementing -strategies-for-the-development.pdf.

CHAPTER 6

1. See, for example, W. V. Fountain, *Academic Sharecroppers: Exploitation of Adjunct Faculty and the Higher Education System* (n.p.: Self-published, 2005).

2. K. N. Shivers, "Adjunct Faculty, Walmart Workers of Higher Education," LinkedIn, April 13, 2015, https://www.linkedin.com/pulse/adjunct-faculty -walmart-workers-education-kaia-shivers.

3. A. Kezar, D. Maxey, and L. Badke, "The Imperative for Change: Fostering Understanding of the Necessity of Changing Non-Tenure-Track Faculty

Policies and Practices," The Delphi Project on the Changing Faculty and Student Success, 2014, https://pullias.usc.edu/download/imperative-change-fostering-understanding-necessity-changing-non-tenure-track-faculty-policies-practices/.

4. Kezar, Maxey, and Badke, "The Imperative for Change."

5. G. Berryman, "The Secret Lives of Adjunct Professors," *Elle*, December 15, 2021, https://www.elle.com/life-love/a38424968/the-secret-lives-of-adjunct-professors/.

6. J. G. Cross and E. N. Goldenberg, *Off-track Profs: Nontenured Teachers in Higher Education* (Cambridge, MA: MIT Press, 2009).

7. J. Harper and A. Kezar, "Systemic Improvement for Teaching Faculty and Expansion of Tenure for Teaching at Worcester Polytechnic Institute (WPI)," The Delphi Project on the Changing Faculty and Student Success, University of Southern California Pullias Center, 2021, https://pullias.usc.edu/wp-content/uploads/2021/12/WPI_Case-udy_Final2021.pdf.

8. D. Ulrich, D. Kryscynski, M. Ulrich, and W. Brockbank, *Victory through Organization: Why the War for Talent Is Failing Your Company and What You Can Do about It* (New York: McGraw Hill, 2017).

9. E. Chun and A. Evans, "Designing and Implementing Strategies for a Winning Faculty Workforce," TIAA-CREF Institute, 2014, https://www.tiaainstitute.org/sites/default/files/presentations/2017-02/designing-and-implementing-strategies-for-the-development.pdf.

10. See A. Evans and E. Chun, *Creating a Tipping Point: Strategic Human Resources in Higher Education*, ASHE Higher Education Report 38, no. 1 (San Francisco: Jossey-Bass, 2012).

11. A. Pritchard and A. Schmidt, "The Higher Ed HR Workforce," College and University Professional Association for Human Resources, https://www.cupahr.org/surveys/research-briefs/2020-the-higher-ed-hr-workforce/.

12. Evans and Chun, *Creating a Tipping Point*; and Ulrich et al., *Victory through Organization*.

13. See, for example, D. Ulrich, W. Brockbank, D. Johnson, K. Sandholtz, and J. Younger, *HR Competencies: Mastery at the Intersection of People and Business* (Alexandria, VA: Society for Human Resource Management, 2008); D. Ulrich, S. Kerr, and R. Ashkenazy, *The GE Work-out: How to Implement GE's Revolutionary Method for Busting Bureaucracy and Attacking Organizational Problems—Fast!* (New York: McGraw-Hill, 2002); and Ulrich et al., *Victory through Organization*.

14. Chun and Evans, "Designing and Implementing Strategies."

15. Ulrich et al., *Victory through Organization*.

16. Ulrich et al., *Victory through Organization*.

17. Chun and Evans, "Designing and Implementing Strategies."

18. American Association of University Professors, "The Annual Report on the Economic Status of the Profession, 2020–2021," July 2021, https://www .aaup.org/file/AAUP_ARES_2020-21.pdf.

19. T. Kolbe and R. Staisloff, "Moving to Offense: A New Playbook for Confronting Budget Shortfalls," Inside Higher Ed, August 6, 2020, https://www .insidehighered.com/views/2020/08/06/new-playbook-confronting-higher -education's-looming-budget-shortfalls-opinion.

20. T. Winders and C. Laux, "An Institutional Approach to Six Sigma in Higher Education," Purdue Polytechnic, accessed January 2, 2022, https://docs.lib purdue.edu/cgi/viewcontent.cgi?article=1019&context=iclss.

21. See, for example, S. Yorkstone, ed., *Global Lean for Higher Education: A Themed Anthology of Case Studies, Approaches, and Tools* (New York: Routledge, 2020); and J. Antony, R. Sreedharan V, and A. Chakraborty, eds., *Lean Six Sigma for Higher Education: Research and Practice* (Covent Garden, UK: World Scientific Publishing, 2020).

22. T. C. Krehbiel, A. W. Ryan, and D. P. Miller, "Miami University Lean: A Case Study Documenting the Lean Journey of Miami University in Oxford, Ohio," accessed January 2, 2022, https://www.miamioh.edu/fbs/lean/lean -articles/index.html.

23. Miami University, Finance and Business Services, "Lean Statistics," accessed January 2, 2022, https://www.miamioh.edu/fbs/lean/lean-statistics /index.html.

24. E. J. Stone, "What's It Like to 'Retire from Nowhere,'" *Chronicle of Higher Education,* December 8, 2021, https://www.chronicle.com/article/what-its -like-to-retire-from-nowhere.

25. University Council–American Federation of Teachers, "2021–2026 Teaching Faculty Contract," accessed January 4, 2022, https://ucaft.org/content /2021-2026-teaching-faculty-contract-summary.

26. J. M. Schwartz, "Resisting the Exploitation of Contingent Faculty Labor in the Neoliberal University: The Challenge of Building Solidarity between Tenured and Non-Tenured Faculty," *New Political Science* 36, no. 4 (2014): 504–22.

27. "Collective Bargaining Agreement between the University of Oregon and United Academics, AAUP/AFT, AFL-CIO, July 1, 2018 through June 30, 2021," accessed January 4, 2022, https://www.uauoregon.org/wp-content/uploads/2021/03/CBA-2021.pdf.

28. D. Paulson, "The End of the Oregon University System," *Eugene Weekly*, July 9, 2015, http://eugeneweekly.com/2015/07/09/the-end-of-the-oregon-university-system/.

29. K. Hand, "United Academics of the University of Oregon," American Association of University Professors, Fall 2020), https://www.aaup.org/article/united-academics-university-oregon#.YdRzTmjMI2w.

30. C. Morphew, K. Ward, and L. Wolf-Wendel, "Contingent Faculty Composition and Utilization: Perspectives from Independent Colleges and Universities," in *Hidden and Visible: The Role and Impact of Contingency Faculty in Higher Education,* ed. J. Naughton, H. A. Garcia, and K. Nehls, 67–81 (Hoboken, NJ: Wiley, 2017).

31. American Federation of Teachers, "An Army of Temps: AFT 2020 Adjunct Faculty Quality of Work/Life Report," 2020, https://www.aft.org/sites/default/files/adjuncts_qualityworklife2020.pdf.

32. J. Jean, "Diversity and the Exploitation of Adjunct Professors: Grown Your Own," Solstice, accessed January 5, 2022, https://solsticelitmag.org/blog/diversity-exploitiation-adjunct-professors/.

33. T. Kraft, "Adjunctification: Living in the Margins of Academe," in *Critical Digital Pedagogy: A Collection*, ed. J. Stommel, C. Friend, and S. M. Morris, chap. 17, https://cdpcollection.pressbooks.com/chapter/adjunctification-living-in-the-margins-of-academe/.

BIBLIOGRAPHY

Allen, D., and G. C. Wolniak. "Exploring the Effects of Tuition Increases on Racial/Ethnic Diversity at Public Colleges and Universities." *Research in Higher Education* 60 (2019): 18–43.

American Association of University Professors. "The Annual Report on the Economic Status of the Profession, 2020–2021." July 2021. https://www.aaup.org/file/AAUP_ARES_2020-21.pdf.

American Association of University Professors. "Background Facts on Contingent Faculty Positions." Accessed January 3, 2022. https://www.aaup.org/issues/contingency/background-facts.

American Association of University Professors. "The Inclusion in Governance of Faculty Members Holding Contingent Appointments." Accessed August 7, 2021. https://www.aaup.org/report/inclusion-governance-faculty-members-holding-contingent-appointments.

American Association of University Professors. "Preliminary Report of the Special Committee on Academic Freedom and Florida." May 24, 2023. https://www.aaup.org/file/Preliminary_Report_Florida.pdf.

American Association of University Professors. "Statement on Legislation Restricting Teaching about Race." August 4, 2021. https://www.aaup.org/news/statement-legislation-restricting-teaching-about-race.

American Association of University Professors, The New School. "New School Imposes Austerity, Slashes Vital and Vulnerable Staff." October 5, 2020. https://www.thenewschoolaaup.org/actions/oct05-press-statement.

American Council on Education. "Comprehensive Demographic Profile of American College Presidents Shows Slow Progress in Diversifying Leadership Ranks, Concerns about Funding." June 20, 2017. https://www.acenet.edu/News-Room/Pages/Comprehensive-Demographic-Profile-of-American-College-Presidents-Shows-Slow-Progress-in-Diversifying-Leadership-Ranks.aspx.

American Federation of Teachers. "An Army of Temps: AFT 2020 Adjunct Faculty Quality of Work/Life Report." Accessed January 8, 2022. https://www.aft.org/sites/default/files/adjuncts_qualityworklife2020.pdf.

American Federation of Teachers. "New Jersey Adjunct Fired after Speaking Out." June 28, 2017. https://www.aft.org/news/new-jersey-adjunct-fired -after-speaking-out.

Antony, J., R. Sreedharan V, and A. Chakraborty, eds. *Lean Six Sigma for Higher Education: Research and Practice.* Covent Garden, UK: World Scientific Publishing, 2020.

Aryee, S., P. S. Budhwar, and Z. X. Chen. "Trust as a Mediator of the Relationship between Organizational Justice and Work Outcomes: Test of a Social Exchange Model." *Journal of Organizational Behavior* 23 (2002): 267–85.

Austin-Hilary, N., and V. Strang. "Racism's Prominent Role in January 6 US Capitol Attack," Human Rights Watch, January 5, 2022. https://www.hrw .org/news/2022/01/05/racisms-prominent-role-january-6-us-capitol-attack.

Bardia, A., S. Yadav, R. Kalpa, and A. Sg. "The New School Is in Crisis." *Jacobin Magazine,* December 20. https://jacobinmag.com/2020/12/the-new-school -nssr-austerity-covid-neoliberalism.

Bauman, D. "After a Year of Losses, Higher Ed's Workforce Is Growing Again." *Chronicle of Higher Education,* July 8, 2021. https://www.chronicle.com/article /after-a-year-of-losses-higher-eds-work-force-is-growing-again.

Bauman, D. "Brutal Tally: Higher Ed Lost 650,000 Jobs Last Year." *Chronicle of Higher Education,* February 5, 2021. https://www.chronicle.com/article/a -brutal-tally-higher-ed-lost-650-000-jobs-last-year.

Bauman, D. "Here's Who Was Hardest Hit by Higher Ed's Pandemic-Driven Job Losses." *Chronicle of Higher Education,* April 19, 2021. https://www .chronicle.com/article/heres-who-was-hit-hardest-by-higher-eds-pandemic -driven-job-losses.

Bavishi, A., J. M. Madera, and M. R. Hebl. "The Effect of Professor Ethnicity and Gender on Student Evaluations: Judged before Met." *Journal of Diversity in Higher Education* 3, no. 4 (2010): 245–56.

Bell, D. "Epilogue: Affirmative Action; Another Instance of Racial Workings in the United States." *Journal of Negro Education* 69, nos. 1–2 (2000): 93–99.

Bella, T. "DeSantis Invokes MLK as He Proposes Stop Woke Act against Critical Race Theory." *Washington Post,* December 15, 2021. https://www .washingtonpost.com/politics/2021/12/15/desantis-stop-woke-act-mlk-crt/.

Bellafante, G. "This School Was Built for Idealists. It Could Use Some Rich Alumni." *New York Times,* October 18, 2020. https://www.nytimes.com /2020/10/16/nyregion/new-school-nyc-endowment-layoffs.html?referring Source=articleShare.

Berryman, G. "The Secret Lives of Adjunct Professors." *Elle*, December 15, 2021. https://www.elle.com/life-love/a38424968/the-secret-lives-of-adjunct -professors/.

Bichsel, J., M. Fuesting, S. Nadel-Hawthorne, and A. Schmidt. *Faculty in Higher Education Annual Report: Key Findings, Trends, and Comprehensive Tables for Tenure-Track, Non-Tenure Teaching, and Non-Tenure Research Faculty and Summary Data for Adjunct Faculty for the 2020–21 Academic Year.* CUPA-HR, March 2021. https://www.cupahr.org/wp-content/uploads /surveys/Results/2021_Faculty_Annual_Report_Overview.pdf.

Blow, C. M. "White Racial Anxiety Strikes Again." *New York Times*, November 3, 2021. https://www.nytimes.com/2021/11/03/opinion/youngkin-virginia -race.html.

Bolitzer, L. A. "What We Know (and Don't Know) about Adjunct Faculty at Four Year Institutions." *Review of Higher Education* 43, no. 1 (2019): 113–42.

Bonner, F. A., II. "'Mascu'sectionality: Theorizing an Alternative Framework for Black Males." Diverse Education, January 19, 2019. https://www.diverse education.com/demographics/african-american/article/15103947 /mascusectionality-theorizing-an-alternative-framework-for-black-males.

Boyer, E. L. *Scholarship Reconsidered: Priorities of the Professoriate.* Princeton, NJ: Carnegie Foundation for the Advancement of Teaching, 1990.

Brennan, J., and P. W. Magness. "Are Adjunct Faculty Exploited: Some Grounds for Skepticism." *Journal of Business Ethics* 152 (2016): 53–71.

Bresciani Lukvik, M. J. *Outcomes-Based Program Review: Closing Achievement Gaps In- and Outside the Classroom with Alignment to Predictive Analytics and Performance Metrics.* 2nd ed. Sterling, VA: Stylus Publishing, 2018.

Brownstein, R. "American Higher Education Hits a Dangerous Milestone." *The Atlantic*, May 3, 2018. https://www.theatlantic.com/politics/archive/2018/05 /american-higher-education-hits-a-dangerous-milestone/559457/.

Burawoy, M. "The Extended Case Method." In *Ethnography Unbound: Power and Resistance in the Modern Metropolis*, ed. M. Burawoy et al., 271–87. Berkeley: University of California Press, 1991.

Burawoy, M. "Reconstructing Social Theories." In *Ethnography Unbound: Power and Resistance in the Modern Metropolis*, ed. M. Burawoy et al., 8–28. Berkeley: University of California Press, 1991.

Busch, L. *Knowledge for Sale: The Neoliberal Takeover of Higher Education.* Cambridge, MA: MIT Press, 2017.

Calma, A., and C. Dickson-Deane. "The Student as Customer and Quality in

Higher Education." *International Journal of Educational Management* 34, no. 8 (2020): 1221–35.

Calvan, B. C. "Florida Bans 'Critical Race Theory' from Its Classrooms." Associated Press, June 10, 2021. https://apnews.com/article/florida-race-and -ethnicity-government-and-politics-education-74d0af6c52c0009ec3fa3ee 9955b0a8d.

Campbell, A. "The Birth of Neoliberalism in the United States: A Reorganisation of Capitalism." In *Neoliberalism: A Critical Reader*, ed. A. Saad-Filho and D. Johnston, 187–98. Ann Arbor, MI: Pluto, 2005.

Carlson, S., E. Hoover, B. McMurtie, E. Pettit, and M. Zahneis. "Forced Out: The Faces of Higher Ed's Layoffs." *Chronicle of Higher Education*, April 21, 2021. https://www.chronicle.com/article/forced-out.

Chang, C. "How the Pandemic Has Pushed Contingent Faculty to the Precipice." *The Best Schools*, June 5, 2020. Accessed April 4, 2021. https://thebestschools .org/magazine/adjunct-layoffs-due-to-covid-19/.

Cheney-Rice, Z. "The Right's New Reason to Panic about 'Critical Race Theory' Is Centuries Old." *New York Magazine*, June 30, 2021. https://nymag.com /intelligencer/2021/06/the-white-panic-behind-critical-race-theory.html.

Chesler, M. A. "The State of Research with Faculty Identities in Higher Educational Classrooms and Institutional Contexts." In *Faculty Identities and the Challenge of Diversity: Reflections on Teaching in Higher Education*, ed. M. A. Chesler and A. A. Young Jr., 1–20. New York: Routledge, 2013.

Chesler, M. A., and A. A. Young Jr., eds. *Faculty Identities and the Challenges of Diversity: Reflections on Teaching in Higher Education*. Boulder, CO: Paradigm Publishers, 2013.

Childress, H. *The Adjunct Underclass: How America's Colleges Betrayed Their Faculty, Their Students, and Their Mission*. Chicago University of Chicago Press, 2019.

Chun, E., and A. Evans. *Bridging the Diversity Divide: Globalization and Reciprocal Empowerment in Higher Education*. ASHE Higher Education Report 35, no. 1. San Francisco: Jossey-Bass, 2009.

Chun, E., and A. Evans. "Designing and Implementing Strategies for the Development of a Winning Faculty Workforce." TIAA Institute, 2014. https://www.tiaa.org/content/dam/tiaa/institute/pdf/full-report/2017-02 /designing-and-implementing-strategies-for-the-development.pdf.

Chun, E., and A. Evans. *Leading a Diversity Culture Shift in Higher Education: Comprehensive Organizational Learning Strategies*. New York: Routledge, 2018.

Chun E., and A. Evans. *Leveraging Multigenerational Workforce Strategies in Higher Education*. New York: Routledge, 2021.

Chun, E. B., and J. R. Feagin. *Rethinking Diversity Frameworks in Higher Education*. New York: Routledge, 2020.

Chun, E. B., and J. R. Feagin. *Who Killed Higher Education? Maintaining White Dominance in a Desegregating Era*. New York: Routledge, 2022.

Coalition of Rutgers Unions. "Rutgers Unions Say 'the Clock Is Ticking' on Another Chance to Stop Layoffs and Cuts." Insider NJ, February 24, 2021. https://www.insidernj.com/press-release/rutgers-unions-say-clock-ticking-another-chance-stop-layoffs-cuts/.

Colby, G. *Data Snapshot: Tenure and Contingency in US Higher Education*. American Association of University Professors, 2023. https://www.aaup.org/sites/default/files/AAUP%20Data%20Snapshot.pdf.

"Collective Bargaining Agreement between the University of Oregon and United Academics, AAUP/AFT, AFL-CIO, July 1, 2018 through June 30, 2021." University of Oregon, 2010. https://www.uauoregon.org/wp-content/uploads/2021/03/CBA-2021.pdf.

College and University Professional Association for Human Resources. "Administrative Compensation Survey: For the 2009–10 Academic Year."

Collins, P. H. *Intersectionality as Critical Social Theory*. Durham, NC: Duke University Press, 2019.

Collins, P. H. "Learning from the Outsider Within: The Sociological Significance of Black Feminist Thought." In *Women in Higher Education: A Feminist Perspective*, ed. J. S. Glazer-Raymo, E. M. Bensimon, and B. K. Townsend, 45–64. Needham Heights, MA: Ginn, 1993.

Cooper, J. E., A. M. Ortiz, M. K. P. Benham, and M. W. Scherr. "Finding a Home in the Academy: Confronting Racism and Ageism." In *Tenure in the Sacred Grove: Issues and Strategies for Women and Minority Faculty*, ed. J. E. Cooper and D. D. Stevens, 71–88. Albany: State University of New York Press, 2002.

Cottom, T. M. "The New Old Labor Crisis." *Slate*, January 24, 2014. https://slate.com/human-interest/2014/01/adjunct-crisis-in-higher-ed-an-all-too-familiar-story-for-black-faculty.html.

Crenshaw, K. "Demarginalizing the Intersection of Race and Sex: A Black Feminist Critique of Antidiscrimination Doctrine, Feminist Theory and Antiracist Politics." *University of Chicago Legal Forum* 1989, no. 1 (1989): Article 8, http://chicagounbound.uchicago.edu/uclf/vol1989/iss1/8.

Crocker, J., K. Vole, M. Test, and B. Major. "Social Stigma: The Affective Consequences of Attributional Ambiguity." *Journal of Personality and Social Psychology* 60, no. 2 (1991): 218–28.

Cross, J. G., and E. N. Goldenberg, *Off-track Profs: Nontenured Teachers in Higher Education.* Cambridge, MA: MIT Press(2009).

Crow, M. M., and W. B. Dabars. *Designing the New American University.* Baltimore: Johns Hopkins University Press, 2015.

Darden, M. L. *Entrepreneuring the Future of Higher Education: Radical Transformation in Times of Profound Change.* Lanham, MD: Rowman & Littlefield, 2021.

Davis, L., and R. Fry. "College Faculty Have Become More Racially and Ethnically Diverse, but Remain Far Less So Than Students." Pew Research Center, July 31, 2019. https://www.pewresearch.org/fact-tank/2019/07/31/us-college-faculty-student-diversity/.

Del Gandio, J. "Neoliberalism, Higher Education, and the Rise of Contingent Faculty Labor." *Public Eye Magazine*, October 15, 2014. https://politicalresearch.org/2014/10/15/neoliberalism-higher-education-and-the-rise-of-contingent-faculty-labor.

The Delphi Project. "National Trends for Faculty Composition over Time." Pullias Center for Higher Education, University of Southern California, 2013. https://pullias.usc.edu/download/national-trends-faculty-composition-time/.

Dhillon, J., C. Arruzza, and AAUP-TNS Media Collective. "Corporate Consultants Set Their Targets on American Universities." *The Nation*, October 23, 2020. https://www.thenation.com/article/society/new-school-huron/.

Dougherty, K. J., and R. S. Natow. "Analysing Neoliberalism in Theory and Practice: The Case of Performance-Based Funding for Higher Education." Working paper no. 44. London: Centre for Global Higher Education, March 2019.

Douglas-Gabriel, D., and A. Fowers. "The Lowest Paid Workers in Higher Education Are Suffering the Highest Job Losses." *Washington Post*, November 17, 2020. https://www.washingtonpost.com/education/2020/11/17/higher-ed-job-loss/.

Drozdowski, M. J. "The Plight of Adjunct Faculty on America's Campuses." BestColleges.com, February 7, 2022. https://www.bestcolleges.com/blog/plight-of-adjunct-faculty/.

Dzhanova, Y. "The Creator of the 1619 Project Is Considering Bringing a Discrimination Lawsuit against UNC after She Was Denied Tenure." *Business*

Insider, May 29, 2010. https://www.nytimes.com/2021/05/19/business/media/nikole-hannah-jones-unc.html?referringSource=articleShare.

Edwards, K., and K. Tolley. "Do Unions Help Adjuncts?" *Chronicle of Higher Education*, June 3, 2018. https://www.chronicle.com/article/do-unions-help-adjuncts/.

Elsen-Rooney, M. "CUNY Board of Trustees Tables Vote on $3 Million Proposal after Criticism." *New York Daily News*, April 12, 2021. https://www.nydailynews.com/new-york/education/ny-cuny-mckinsey-reopening-plan-20210412-mogeiwjko5dgpdql3l3d2rsvyi-story.html.

Evans, A., and E. B. Chun. *Are the Walls Really Down? Behavioral and Organizational Barriers to Faculty and Staff Diversity*. San Francisco: Jossey-Bass, 2007.

Evans, A., and E. Chun, *Creating a Tipping Point: Strategic Human Resources in Higher Education*. ASHE Higher Education Report 38, no. 1. San Francisco: Jossey-Bass, 2012.

Feagin, J. R. *Systemic Racism: A Theory of Oppression*. New York: Routledge, 2006.

Finkelstein, M. J., V. M. Conley, and J. H. Schuster. *The Faculty Factor: Reassessing the American Academy in Turbulence*. Baltimore: Johns Hopkins University Press, 2016.

Finkelstein, M. J., V. M. Conley, and J. H. Schuster. "Taking the Measure of Faculty Diversity." TIAA-CREF Institute, April 2016. https://www.tiaa.org/content/dam/tiaa/institute/pdf/full-report/2017-02/taking-the-measure-of-faculty-diversity.pdf.

Flaherty, C. "'A Blatant Intrusion.'" Inside Higher Ed, May 20, 2021. https://www.insidehighered.com/news/2021/05/20/unc-chapel-hill-board-doesnt-approve-tenure-noted-journalist.

Flaherty, C. "Prioritization Anxiety." Inside Higher Ed, August 16, 2016. https://www.insidehighered.com/news/2016/08/16/how-can-increasingly-popular-academic-review-process-seem-more-meaningful-faculty.

Flaherty, C. "The Skinny on Teaching Evals and Bias." Inside Higher Ed, February 17, 2021. https://www.insidehighered.com/news/2021/02/17/whats-really-going-respect-bias-and-teaching-evals.

Florida College System College of Presidents. "Florida College System Presidents Statement on Diversity, Equity, Inclusion and Critical Race Theory." January 18, 2023. https://www.fldoe.org/core/fileparse.php/5673/urlt/FCSDEIstatement.pdf.

Florida Senate. "CS/CS/CS/SB 266: Higher Education." 2023. https://www.flsenate.gov/Session/Bill/2023/266.

Florida Senate. "HB 57: Racial and Sexual Discrimination." 2022. https://www
.flsenate.gov/Session/Bill/2022/57.

Fountain, W. V. *Academic Sharecroppers: Exploitation of Adjunct Faculty and the
Higher Education System*. n.p.: Self-published, 2005.

Friedman, M. *Capitalism and Freedom*. Chicago University of Chicago Press, 2002.

Fuchs, H. "Trump Attack on Diversity Training Has a Quick and Chilling Effect."
New York Times, October 13, 2020. https://www.nytimes.com/2020/10/13/us
/politics/trump-diversity-training-race.html?referringSource=articleShare.

Fulk, A. B. "Confronting Biases against Adjunct Faculty." Inside Higher Ed,
February 14, 2019. https://www.insidehighered.com/advice/2019/02/14/how
-bias-toward-adjuncts-plays-out-among-students-other-faculty-and
-administrators.

Gappa, J. M. "The Stress-Producing Working Conditions of Part-Time Faculty." In *Coping with Faculty Stress*, ed. P. Seldin, 33–42. San Francisco:
Jossey-Bass, 1987.

Gappa, J. M., A. E., Austin, and A. G. Trice. *Rethinking Faculty Work: Higher
Education's Strategic Imperative*. San Francisco: Jossey-Bass, 2007.

Gappa, J. M., and D. W. Leslie. *The Invisible Faculty: Improving the Status of
Part-Timers in Higher Education*. San Francisco: Jossey-Bass, 1993.

Gehrke, S., and A. Kezar. "Understanding the Faculty Role in Higher Education:
Utilizing Historical, Theoretical, and Empirical Frameworks to Inform Future Research." In *Higher Education: Handbook of Theory and Research*, ed.
M. B. Paulsen, 93–150. Cham, Switzerland: Springer International Publishing, 2015.

Giroux, H. A. *Neoliberalism's War on Higher Education*. Chicago: Haymarket
Books, 2014.

Goez, J. R. "Exploring How an Academic Institution Implements a Diversity,
Equity, and Inclusion Initiative in a Non-Tenure-Track Environment." PhD
dissertation, Teachers College, Columbia University, 2021.

Goh, J., J. Pfeffer, and S. Zenios. "The Relationship between Workplace Stressors
and Mortality and Health Costs in the United States." *Management Science*
62 (2016): 608–28.

Goist, R. "Arbitrator Sides with University of Akron in Layoff of Nearly 100
Union Faculty." Cleveland.com, September 18, 2020. https://www.cleveland
.com/education/2020/09/arbitrator-sides-with-university-of-akron-in
-layoff-of-nearly-100-union-faculty.html.

Gregory, R. F. *Age Discrimination in the American Workplace: Old at a Young Age*.
Piscataway, NJ: Rutgers University Press, 2001.

Hall, G. *The Uberfication of the University*. Minneapolis: University of Minnesota Press, 2016.

Hand, K. *United Academics of the University of Oregon*. American Association of University Professors, Fall 2020. https://www.aaup.org/article/united -academics-university-oregon#.YdRzTmjMI2w.

Harper, J., and A. Kezar. "Systemic Improvement for Teaching Faculty and Expansion of Tenure for Teaching at Worcester Polytechnic Institute (WPI)." The Delphi Project on the Changing Faculty and Student Success, University of Southern California Pullias Center, 2021. https://pullias.usc.edu /wp-content/uploads/2021/12/WPI_Case-Study_Final2021.pdf.

Harris, A. "The Death of an Adjunct." *The Atlantic*, April 9, 2019. https://www. theatlantic.com/education/archive/2019/04/adjunct-professors-higher -education-thea-hunter/586168/.

Hartlep, N. D., and D. Ball. "The Battle of Racial Battle Fatigue." In *Racial Battle Fatigue in Faculty: Perspectives and Lessons from Higher Education*, ed. N. D. Hartlep and D. Ball, 1–13. New York: Routledge, 2020.

Harvey, D. *A Brief History of Neoliberalism*. Oxford: Oxford University Press, 2007.

Hodges, C. R., and O. M. Welch. "Making Noise and Good, Necessary Trouble: Dilemmas of 'Deaning While Black.'" In *Dismantling Institutional Whiteness: Emerging Forms of Leadership in Higher Education*, ed. M. C. Alcade and M. Subramaniam, 55–77. West Lafayette, IN: Purdue University Press, 2023.

Hohle, R. *Race and the Origins of American Neoliberalism*. New York: Routledge, 2015.

Hohle, R. *Racism in the Neoliberal Era: A Meta History of Elite White Power*. New York: Routledge, 2018.

Huelsman, M. "Social Exclusion: The State of State U for Black Students." Demos, 2018. www.demos.org/research/social-exclusion-state-state-u-black-students.

Huron. "University of New Hampshire Executive Summary: Resource Assessment and Academic Program Cost." University of New Hampshire, March 3, 2020. https://www.unh.edu/sites/default/files/unh_plc_huron_findings _final_updated_3.3.20.pdf.

Ibarra, H., N. M. Carter, and C. Silva. "Why Men Still Get More Promotions Than Women." *Harvard Business Review* 88, no. 9 (September 2010): 80–126.

Jackson, V., and M. Saenz. *States Can Choose Better Path for Higher Education Funding in Covid-19 Recession*. Center on Budget and Policy Priorities, February 17, 2021. https://www.cbpp.org/research/state-budget-and-tax/states -can-choose-better-path-for-higher-education-funding-in-covid.

Jean, J. "Diversity and the Exploitation of Adjunct Professors: Grown Your

Own." *Solstice.* Accessed January 5, 2022. https://solsticelitmag.org/blog
/diversity-exploitiation-adjunct-professors/.

Joseph, T. D., and L. Hirshfield. "'Why don't you get somebody new to do
it?' Race, Gender, and Identity Taxation." In *Faculty Social Identity and the
Challenges of Diverse Classrooms in A Historically White University,* ed. M. Chesler and A. A. Young Jr., 153–69. Boulder, CO: Paradigm Publishers, 2013.

June, A. W. "Job Cuts and Stagnant Salaries: A New Report Details the Pandemic's Toll on the Faculty." *Chronicle of Higher Education,* March 30, 2021.
https://www.chronicle.com/blogs/live-coronavirus-updates/job-cuts-and
-stagnant-salaries-a-new-report-details-the-pandemics-toll-on-the-faculty.

Kang, S. K. "Beyond the Double-Jeopardy Hypothesis: Examining the Interaction between Age- and Race-Based Stereotypes across the Lifespan." PhD
dissertation, University of Toronto, 2010.

Kezar, A. "Departmental Cultures and Non-Tenure-Track Faculty: Willingness,
Capacity, and Opportunity to Perform at Four-Year Institutions." *Journal of
Higher Education* 84, no. 2 (2013): 153–88.

Kezar, A. *How Colleges Change: Understanding, Leading, and Enacting Change.*
New York: Routledge, 2014.

Kezar, A., T. DePaola, and D. T. Scott. *The Gig Academy: Mapping Labor in the
Neoliberal University.* Baltimore: Johns Hopkins University Press, 2019.

Kezar, A., D. Maxey, and L. Badke. "The Imperative for Change: Fostering
Understanding of the Necessity of Changing Non-Tenure-Track Faculty
Policies and Practices." The Delphi Project on the Changing Faculty and
Student Success, 2014. https://pullias.usc.edu/download/imperative
-change-fostering-understanding-necessity-changing-non-tenure-track
-faculty-policies-practices/.

Kezar, A., and C. Sam. "Governance as a Catalyst for Policy Change: Creating
a Contingent Faculty Friendly Academy." *Educational Policy* 28, no. 3 (2014):
425–62.

Kim, K. W., A. Kalev, F. Dobbin, and G. Deutsch. "Crisis and Uncertainty:
Did the Great Recession Reduce the Diversity of New Faculty?" *Sociological
Science* 8 (2020): 308–24.

Koenig, R. "'Academic Capitalism' Is Reshaping Faculty Life. What Does That
Mean?" EdSurge, November 25, 2019. https://www.edsurge.com/news/2019
-11-25-academic-capitalism-is-reshaping-faculty-life-what-does-that-mean.

Kolbe, T., and R. Staisloff. "Moving to Offense: A New Playbook for Confronting
Budget Shortfalls." Inside Higher Ed, August 6, 2020. https://www

.insidehighered.com/views/2020/08/06/new-playbook-confronting-higher
-education's-looming-budget-shortfalls-opinion.

Kraft, T. "Adjunctification: Living in the Margins of Academe." In *Critical Digital Pedagogy: A Collection*, ed. J. Stommel, C. Friend, and S. M. Morris, chap. 17. Pressbooks, 2020. https://cdpcollection.pressbooks.com/chapter/adjunctification-living-in-the-margins-of-academe/.

Krantz, L. "In Higher Education, the Pandemic Has Been Especially Cruel to Adjunct Professors." *Boston Globe*, September 20, 2020. https://www.boston globe.com/2020/09/20/metro/pandemic-deepens-great-divide-academia/.

Krehbiel, T. C., A. W. Ryan, and D. P. Miller. "Miami University Lean: A Case Study Documenting the Lean Journey of Miami University in Oxford, Ohio." Accessed January 2, 2022. https://www.miamioh.edu/fbs/lean/lean-articles/index.html.

Kreitzer, R. J., and J. Sweet-Cushman. "Evaluating Student Evaluations of Teaching: A Review of Measurement and Equity Bias in SETs and Recommendations for Ethical Reform." *Journal of Academic Ethics* 20, no. 1 (2021): 73–84.

Kunstman, J. W., T. Tuscherer, S. Trawalter, and E. P. Lloyd. "What Lies Beneath? Minority Group Members' Suspicion of Whites' Egalitarian Motivation Predicts Responses to Whites' Smiles." *Personality and Social Psychology Bulletin* 42, no. 9 (2016): 1193–205.

Laderman, S., and T. Harnisch. "Analysis of Federal Stimulus Funding to States and Public Institutions of Higher Education." State Higher Education Executive Officers Association, 2021. https://shef.sheeo.org/wp-content/uploads/2021/05/SHEEO_SHEF_FY20_IB_Federal_Stimulus.pdf.

Lang, C. "President Trump Has Attacked Critical Race Theory. Here's What to Know about the Intellectual Movement." *Time*, September 29, 2020. https://time.com/5891138/critical-race-theory-explained/.

Lazarus, R. S. "Theory-Based Stress Management." *Psychological Inquiry* 1, no. 1 (1990): 3–13.

Lebbaeus, A. A., and O. Mensah. "To What Extent Does Employees' Perception of Organizational Justice Influence Their Organizational Citizenship Behaviour?" *European Journal of Business and Management* 5, no. 16 (2013): 32–41.

Leddy, C. "CUNY Leaders Pressed on Thousands of Faculty Layoffs." *Gotham Gazette*, November 13, 2020. https://www.gothamgazette.com/state/9905-cuny-leaders-pressed-layoffs-adjuncts-professors-city-council.

Leonard, J., and N. Cook. "Biden Says 'White Supremacy' Drove Trump's

January 6 Rioters." Bloomberg, October 21, 2021. https://www.bloomberg
.com/news/articles/2021-10-21/biden-says-white-supremacy-motivated
-trump-s-jan-6-rioters.

Liu, J. "A Record 4.4 Million People Quit in September as Great Resignation
Shows No Signs of Stopping." CNBC, November 12, 2021. https://www
.cnbc.com/2021/11/12/a-record-4point4-million-people-quit-jobs-in
-september-great-resignation.html.

Lovelli, B. "University Officials Push Back against Proposed Budget Cuts."
Honolulu Civil Beat, May 6, 2021. https://www.civilbeat.org/2021/05
/university-of-hawaii-officials-push-back-against-proposed-budget-cuts/.

Magness, P. W. "For-Profit Universities and the Roots of Adjunctification in US
Higher Education." *Liberal Education* (Spring 2016): 50–59.

Malinowitz, H. "The Faces of Austerity." *The Ithacan*, February 8, 2021. https://
theithacan.org/news/the-faces-of-austerity-feb-18/.

Maxey, D., and A. Kezar. "The Current Context for Faculty Work in Higher
Education: Understanding the Forces Affecting Higher Education and the
Changing Faculty." In *Envisioning the Faculty for the Twenty-First Century:
Moving to A Mission-Oriented and Learner-Centered Model*, ed. D. Maxey and
A. Kezar, 3–22. New Brunswick, NJ: Rutgers University Press, 2016.

Maxey, D., and A. Kezar. "Revealing Opportunities and Obstacles for Changing
Non-Tenure-Track Faculty Practices: An Examination of Stakeholders'
Awareness of Institutional Contradictions." *Journal of Higher Education* 86,
no. 4 (2015): 564–94.

McClendon, M. K., J. C. Hearn, and C. J. Mokher. "Partisans, Professionals, and
Power: The Role of Political Factors in State Higher Education Funding."
Journal of Higher Education 80, no. 6 (2009): 686–713.

McConnell, B. "'A Blatant Disregard': UNC Journalism Faculty Criticize Trustees for Hannah-Jones Controversy." Chapelboro.com, June 4, 2021. https://
chapelboro.com/news/unc/a-blatant-disregard-unc-journalism-faculty
-criticize-trustees-for-hannah-jones-controversy.

McKinsey & Company. "Winning with Your Talent Management Strategy." 2018.
https://www.mckinsey.com/business-functions/people-and-organizational
-performance/our-insights/winning-with-your-talent-management-strategy.

McKinsey & Company. "Women in the Workplace 2021." Accessed December
2, 2021. https://www.mckinsey.com/~/media/mckinsey/featured%20insights
/diversity%20and%20inclusion/women%20in%20the%20workplace%202021
/women-in-the-workplace-2021.pdf.

Mercatus Center. "About." George Mason University. Accessed June 22, 2020. www.mercatus.org/about#:~:text=Our%20mission%20is%20to%20generate ,%2C%20prosperous%2C%20and%20peaceful%20lives.

Metcalf, A. S., and S. Slaughter. "The Differential Effects of Academic Capitalism on Women in the Academy." In *Unfinished Agendas: New and Continuing Gender Challenges in Higher Education*, ed. J. Glazer-Raymo, 80–111. Baltimore: Johns Hopkins University Press, 2008.

Miami University, Finance and Business Services. "Lean Statistics." Accessed January 2, 2022. https://www.miamioh.edu/fbs/lean/lean-statistics/index.html.

Minor, J. T. "Faculty Diversity and the Traditions of Academic Governance." In *Measuring Glass Ceiling Effects in Higher Education: Opportunities and Challenges*, ed. J. F. L. Jackson, E. M. O'Callaghan, and R. A. Leon, 49–61. San Francisco: Jossey-Bass, 2014.

Mintz, B. "Neoliberalism and the Crisis in Higher Education: The Cost of Ideology." *American Journal of Economics and Sociology* 80, no. 1 (2021): 79–112.

Morphew, C., K. Ward, and L. Wolf-Wendel. "Contingent Faculty Composition and Utilization: Perspectives from Independent Colleges and Universities." In *Hidden and Visible: The Role and Impact of Contingency Faculty in Higher Education*, ed. J. Naughton, H. A. Garcia, and K. Nehls, 67–81. Hoboken, NJ: Wiley, 2017.

Mortenson, T. G. "State Funding: A Race to the Bottom." American Council on Education, 2012. https://www.acesconnection.com/g/aces-in-education /blog/state-funding-a-race-to-the-bottom-american-council-on-education.

Museus, S. D., and K. A. Griffin. "Mapping the Margins in Higher Education: On the Promise of Intersectionality Frameworks in Research and Discourse." In *Using Mixed-Methods Approaches to Study Intersectionality in Higher Education*, ed. K. A. Griffin and S. D. Museus, 5–13. San Francisco: Wiley, 2011.

National Association of College and University Business Officers. "National Profile of Higher Education Business Officers Released." August 9, 2021. https://www.nacubo.org/Press-Releases/2021/National-Profile-of-Higher -Education-Chief-Business-Officers-Released.

National Association of College and University Business Officers. "2021 National Profile of Higher Education Chief Business Officers." 2021. https:// www.nacubo.org/-/media/Documents/Research/2021-National-Profile-of -Higher-Education-Chief-Business-OfficersRevised1221.ash.

National Center for Education Statistics. "The Condition of Education 2020." Accessed April 25, 2021. https://nces.ed.gov/programs/coe/summary.asp.

National Center for Education Statistics. "Table 324.20. Doctor's Degrees Conferred by Postsecondary Institutions, by Race/Ethnicity and Sex of Student: Selected Years, 1976–77 through 2014–15." *Digest of Education Statistics.* Accessed April 25, 2021. https://nces.ed.gov/programs/digest/d16/tables /dt16_324.20.asp.

National Education Association. "Corona Virus Relief for Higher Education Toolkit." April 15, 2021. https://www.nea.org/resource-library/higher -education-covid-19-relief-briefing.

Naughton, J., H. A. Garcia, and K. Nehls. "Understanding the Growth of Contingent Faculty." In *Hidden and Visible: The Role and Impact of Contingency Faculty in Higher Education*, ed. J. Naughton, H. A. Garcia, and K. Nehls, 9–26. New Directions in Institutional Research, 76. Hoboken, NJ: Wiley, 2017.

Nierenberg, A. "What Does 'Don't Say Gay' Actually Say?" *New York Times*, March 23, 2022. https://www.nytimes.com/2022/03/23/us/what-does-dont -say-gay-actually-say.html.

Newfield, C. *The Great Mistake: How We Wrecked Public Universities and How We Can Fix Them.* Baltimore: Johns Hopkins University Press, 2016.

Organization of American Historians. "In Memoriam: Thea K. Hunter." April 25, 2019. https://www.oah.org/insights/archive/in-memoriam-thea-k-hunter.

Paul, A. "Adjuncts Face Dire Situation as CUNY Downsizes." PSC CUNY, December 2020. https://www.psc-cuny.org/clarion/december-2020/adjuncts -face-dire-situation-cuny-downsizes.

Paulson, D. "The End of the Oregon University System." Eugene Weekly, July 9, 2015. http://eugeneweekly.com/2015/07/09/the-end-of-the-oregon -university-system/.

Pettigrew, T. F., and J. Martin. "Shaping the Organizational Context for Black American Inclusion." *Journal of Social Issues* 43, no. 1 (1987): 41–78.

Pettit, E. "'It just felt wrong': U. of Florida Faculty Say Political Fears Stalled an Initiative on Race." *Chronicle of Higher Education*, November 30, 2021. https://www.chronicle.com/article/it-just-felt-wrong-u-of-florida-faculty -say-political-fears-stalled-an-initiative-on-race.

Pfeffer, J. *Dying for A Paycheck: How Modern Management Harms Employee Health and Company Performance—and What We Can Do about It.* New York: HarperCollins, 2018.

Pignolet, J. "Lack of Trust and Fear of Long-Term Damages Loom after University of Akron Faculty Layoffs." *Akron Beacon Journal*, October 24, 2020. https://www.beaconjournal.com/story/news/2020/10/04/faculty-trust

-eroded-after-university-akron-layoffs-covid-19-higher-education/5890230002/.

Porter, C. J., C. M. Moore, G. J. Boss, T. J. Davis, and D. A. Louis. "To Be Black Women and Contingent Faculty: Four Personal Scholarly Narratives." *Journal of Higher Education* 91, no. 5 (2020): 674–97.

Powers, J. B. "Technology Transfer, Commercialization, and Proprietary Science." In *The Business of Higher Education (2): Management and Fiscal Strategies*, ed. J. C. Knapp and D. J. Siegel, 73–95. Santa Barbara, CA: ABC/CLIO-Praeger, 2009.

Prilleltensky, I., and L. Gonick. "The Discourse of Oppression in the Social Sciences: Past, Present, and Future." In *Human Diversity: Perspectives on People in Context*, ed. E. J. Trickett, R. J. Watts, and D. Birman, 145–77. San Francisco: Jossey-Bass, 1994.

Purcell, M. "'Skilled, Cheap, and Desperate': Non-Tenure-Track Faculty and the Delusion of Meritocracy." *Antipode* (2007): 121–43.

Quilantan, B. "Biden's Covid Relief Won't Shield Many Public Colleges from Pandemic's Blow." Politico, March 11, 2021. https://www.politico.com/news/2021/03/11/public-colleges-and-universities-brace-for-steep-budget-cuts-spurred-by-the-pandemic-475393.

Ran, X., and D. Xu. "How and Why Do Adjunct Instructors Affect Students' Academic Outcomes? Evidence from Two-Year and Four-Year Colleges." CAPSEE working paper, Community College Research Center, Teachers College, Columbia University, 2017. https://academiccommons.columbia.edu/doi/10.7916/D80V8JDP.

Reichman, H. "Do Adjuncts Have Academic Freedom? Or Why Tenure Matters: The Costs of Contingency." *Academe* (Winter 2021). https://www.aaup.org/article/do-adjuncts-have-academic-freedom-or-why-tenure-matters#.YdxAFP7MI2w.

Robertson, K. "Nikole Hannah-Jones Denied Tenure at University of North Carolina." *New York Times*, May 19, 2021. https://www.nytimes.com/2021/05/19/business/media/nikole-hannah-jones-unc.html?referringSource=articleShare.

Robertson, K. "Nikole Hannah-Jones Is Granted Tenure after Weekslong Dispute." *New York Times*, June 30, 2021. https://www.nytimes.com/2021/06/30/business/media/nikole-hannah-jones-unc-tenure.html?referringSource=articleShare.

Ropers-Huilman, B. "Women Faculty and the Dance of Identities: Constructing Self and Privilege within Community." In *Unfinished Agendas: New and*

Continuing Gender Challenges in Higher Education, ed. J. Glazer-Raymo, 35–51. Baltimore: Johns Hopkins University Press, 2008.

Roscigno, V. J. "Ageism in the American Workforce." *Contexts* 9 (2010): 16–21.

Roscigno, V. J., S. H. Lopez, and R. Hodson. "Supervisory Bullying, Status Inequalities and Organizational Context." *Social Forces* 87, no. 3 (2009): 1561–89.

Rosenberg, B. "The Deafening Silence of Florida's College Presidents." *Chronicle of Higher Education*, April 6, 2023. https://www.chronicle.com/article/the-deafening-silence-of-floridas-college-presidents.

Samalavičius, A., ed. *Neoliberalism, Economism, and Higher Education.* Newcastle upon Tyne, UK: Cambridge Scholars Publishing, 2018.

Sato, T. C. "Ignored, Pacified, and Deflected: Racial Battle Fatigue for an Asian American Non-Tenure Track Professor." In *Racial Battle Fatigue in Faculty: Perspectives and Lessons from Higher Education*, ed. N. D. Hartlep and D. Ball, 84–98. New York: Routledge, 2019.

Schwartz, J. M. "Resisting the Exploitation of Contingent Faculty Labor in the Neoliberal University: The Challenge of Building Solidarity between Tenured and Non-Tenured Faculty." *New Political Science* 36, no. 4 (2014): 504–22.

Schwartz, S. "Map: Where Critical Race Theory Is under Attack." Education Week, October 28, 2021. https://www.edweek.org/policy-politics/map-where-critical-race-theory-is-under-attack/2021/06.

Shivers, K. N. "Adjunct Faculty, Walmart Workers of Higher Education." LinkedIn, April 13, 2015. https://www.linkedin.com/pulse/adjunct-faculty-walmart-workers-education-kaia-shivers.

Slaughter, S., and G. , *Academic Capitalism and the New Economy: Market, State, and Higher Education.* Baltimore: Johns Hopkins University Press, 2004.

Slaughter, S., and G. Rhoades. "The Neo-liberal University." *New Labor Forum* 6 (2000): 73–79.

Smith, A. M., M. B. Watkins, J. J. Ladge, and P. Carlton. "Interviews with 59 Black Female Executives Explore Intersectional Invisibility and Strategies to Overcome It." *Harvard Business Review*, May 10, 2018. https://hbr.org/2018/05/interviews-with-59-black-female-executives-explore-intersectional-invisibility-and-strategies-to-overcome-it.

Smith, W. A. "Foreword." In *Racial Battle Fatigue in Faculty: Perspectives and Lessons from Higher Education*, ed. N. D. Hartlep and D. Ball, xix–xxii. New York: Routledge, 2020.

Smith, W. A., M. Hung, and J. D. Franklin. "Racial Battle Fatigue and the Mis-education of Black Men: Racial Microaggressions, Societal Problems, and Environmental Stress." *Journal of Negro Education* 80, no. 1 (2011): 63–82.

Starr, P. *Entrenchment: Wealth, Power, and the Constitution of Democratic Societies.* New Haven, CT: Yale University Press, 2019.

State Higher Education Executive Officers Association. "Shef Fy 2020." 2021. https://shef.sheeo.org/wp-content/uploads/2021/05/SHEEO_SHEF_FY20_Report.pdf.

State Higher Education Executive Officers Association. "State Higher Education Finance: Fy 2019." 2020. https://shef.sheeo.org/wp-content/uploads/2020/04/SHEEO_SHEF_FY19_Report.pdf.

Stolzenberg, E. B., et al. "Undergraduate Teaching Faculty: The Heri Faculty Survey 2016–2017." Higher Education Research Institute at UCLA, 2017. https://heri.ucla.edu/monographs/HERI-FAC2017-monograph.pdf.

Stone, E. J. "What's It Like to 'Retire from Nowhere.'" *Chronicle of Higher Education*, December 8, 2021. https://www.chronicle.com/article/what-its-like-to-retire-from-nowhere.

Taylor, B. J., and B. Cantwell. *Unequal Higher Education: Wealth, Status, and Student Opportunity.* New Brunswick, NJ: Rutgers University Press, 2019.

Taylor, B. J., B. Cantwell, K. Watts, and O. Wood. "Partisanship, White Racial Resentment, and State Support for Higher Education." *Journal of Higher Education* 91, no. 6 (2020): 858–87.

Tiede, H-J. "The 2021 AAUP Shared Governance Survey: Findings on Demographics of Senate Chairs and Governance Structures." *Academe*, 2021. https://www.aaup.org/article/2021-aaup-shared-governance-survey-findings-demographics-senate-chairs-and-governance#.YW2GwxrMI2w.

Tolley, K., ed. *Professors in the Gig Economy: Unionizing Adjunct Faculty in America.* Baltimore: Johns Hopkins University Press, 2018.

Tolley, K., and E. Edwards. "Conclusion: Reflections on the Possibilities and Limitations of Collective Bargaining." In *Professors in the Gig Economy: Unionizing Adjunct Faculty in America*, ed. K. Tolley, 187–202. Baltimore: Johns Hopkins University Press, 2018.

Tomaskovic-Dewey, D., and D. Avent-Holt. *Relational Inequalities: An Organizational Approach.* Oxford: Oxford University Press, 2020.

Trump, D. J. "Executive Order on Combating Race and Sex Stereotyping." White House Archives, September 22, 2020. https://trumpwhitehouse.archives.gov/presidential-actions/executive-order-combating-race-sex-stereotyping/.

"UIC UF NTT Job Security Press Conference." YouTube, May 20, 2021. https://www.youtube.com/watch?v=csWKZyFl5UM.

Ulrich, D., W. Brockbank, D. Johnson, K. Sandholtz, and J. Younger. *HR Competencies: Mastery at the Intersection of People and Business*. Alexandria, VA: Society for Human Resource Management, 2008.

Ulrich, D., S. Kerr, and R. Ashkenazy. *The GE Work-Out: How to Implement GE's Revolutionary Method for Busting Bureaucracy and Attacking Organizational Problems-Fast!* New York: McGraw Hill, 2002.

Ulrich, D., D. Kryscynski, M. Ulrich, and W. Brockbank. *Victory through Organization: Why the War for Talent Is Failing Your Company and What You Can Do about It*. New York: McGraw Hill, 2017.

University Council–American Federation of Teachers. "2021–2026 Teaching Faculty Contract." Accessed January 4, 2022. https://ucaft.org/content/2021-2026-teaching-faculty-contract-summary.

University of California, Office of the President. "Academic Personnel and Programs." Accessed August 18, 2021. https://www.ucop.edu/academic-personnel-programs/academic-personnel-policy/appointment-and-promotion/index.html.

University of New Hampshire. "Update No. 17 from President Dean." January 17, 2020. https://www.unh.edu/main/update-no-17-president-dean.

US Department of Education. *Digest of Education Statistics, 2014*. 2014. https://nces.ed.gov/pubs2016/2016006.pdf.

US Department of Education. *Digest of Education Statistics, 2020*. 2020. https://nces.ed.gov/pubsearch/pubsinfo.asp?pubid=2022009.

US Department of Education, National Center for Education Statistics. "Integrated Postsecondary Education Data System." https://nces.ed.gov/ipeds/.

Valbrun, M. "Lives and Livelihoods." Inside Higher Ed, June 23, 2020. https://www.insidehighered.com/news/2020/06/23/cuny-system-suffers-more-coronavirus-deaths-any-other-higher-ed-system-us.

Wallace, S. L., A.K. Lewis, and M. Allen. "The State of the Literature on Student Evaluations of Teaching and an Exploratory Analysis of Written Comments: Who Benefits Most?" *College Teaching* 67, no. 1 (2019): 1–11.

Wallace-Wells, B. "How a Conservative Activist Invented the Conflict over Critical Race Theory." *New Yorker*, June 18, 2021. https://www.newyorker.com/news/annals-of-inquiry/how-a-conservative-activist-invented-the-conflict-over-critical-race-theory.

Whitford, E. "Colleges Could Lose $183 Billion during Pandemic." Inside Higher Ed, February 8, 2021. https://www.insidehighered.com/quicktakes/2021/02/09/colleges-could-lose-183-billion-during-pandemic.

Whitford, E. "How Federal Stimulus Spending Plays Out for State Higher Education." Inside Higher Ed, May 28, 2021. https://www.insidehighered.com/news/2021/05/28/federal-stimulus-higher-ed-replay-2009.

Winders, T., and C. Laux. "An Institutional Approach to Six Sigma in Higher Education." Purdue Polytechnic. Accessed January 2, 2022. https://docs.lib.purdue.edu/cgi/viewcontent.cgi?article=1019&context=iclss.

WXTL. "New Bill Would Ban Critical Race Theory from Florida Public Universities, State Colleges." Accessed December 17, 2021. https://www.wtxl.com/news/local-news/new-bill-would-ban-critical-race-theory-from-florida-public-universities-state-colleges.

Yakoboski, P. "Adjunct Faculty: Who They Are and What Is Their Experience?" TIAA Institute, November 2018. https://www.tiaa.org/public/institute/publication/2018/adjunct-faculty-survey-2018.

Yorkstone, S., ed. *Global Lean for Higher Education: A Themed Anthology of Case Studies, Approaches, and Tools.* New York: Routledge, 2020.

INDEX

Page numbers in italics indicate figures and tables

D

Dabars, William, 123–24
Data Snapshot (Colby), 45
Dean, James W., Jr., 42
defunding of higher education, 2–3, 37, 38. *See also* funding
degrees of inclusion, within university departments, 112–13
DEI. *See* diversity, equity, and inclusion initiatives
Delphi Project on the Changing Faculty and Student Success, 113
democratic society, education and, 26–27, 143–44
demographics: change of racial, 116; of four-year institutions, 45–50
DePaola, Tom, 4
departmental cultures, within universities, 112–14
department chairs: different experience with, 77–78; lack of feedback from, 77; micromanagement by, 77; overreliance on, 62, 129; support of, 79
department culture study, of Kezar, 113–14
departments, curriculum design of, 75–76
DeSantis, Ron, 119, 121; approach to education, 119–20; quoting of M. L. King during bill introduction, 120
Designing the New American University (Crow and Dabars), 123–24
destructive cultures, 113
differential treatment, 67–71, 96–99
difficult topics, employment insecurity and, 79–80, 118–19
discrimination: faced by women of

color, 14, 79–80, 101; lawsuit, 40; relation to stress, UCLA study in, 68; reverse, 23, 82–85
diversity: faculty, 51, 88; initiatives reliance on minoritized faculty for, 65–66; of specialized institutions, 50; strategic plans inclusion of minoritized contingent faculty in, 136; student, 29–32, 130; training, Trump administration on, 115. *See also* diversity, equity, and inclusion (DEI) initiatives
diversity, equity, and inclusion (DEI) initiatives, 109, 119–20, 121–22, 135, 136, 144
divisive climate, of United States, 114–23
doctoral institutions, adjunct faculty at, 46, 49–50
double marginalization, of minoritized contingent faculty, 10–12, 62–63, 106–7, 112–13, 127
Drozdowski, Mark, 61
Dying for a Paycheck (Pfeffer), 6–7

E

economic struggles, of academic underclass, 72–73, 141–42
educational mission, centrality of teaching to, 33–34
Edwards, Kristen, 6, 92–93
elite universities, use of adjunct faculty of, 51
emotional labor, 104
employee experience, human resources research on, 124
employment insecurity, 31, 61–62, 69–70, 89–90, 142; difficult topics and, 79–80, 118–19; Purcell on, 126; semester-by-semester

ABOUT THE AUTHORS

EDNA B. CHUN, DM, SERVES AS CHIEF LEARNING OFFICER WITH HIGHERED Talent and teaches in the graduate Human Capital Management program in the Columbia University School of Professional Studies. She has more than two decades of strategic human resource and diversity leadership experience in public higher education. A sought-after keynote speaker and facilitator, Chun is an award-winning author and thought leader with a major body of published work on diversity and human resource practices in higher education. Her work and publications focus on academic and administrative talent practices that build organizational capacity. As an internationally recognized expert in leadership development, Chun frequently advises universities and colleges on diversity strategic planning, total rewards strategy, talent acquisition and retention, change management and organizational development, cultural competence, inclusive pedagogy, and the integration of diversity and human resources practices. Her particular expertise is in the development of concrete research-based strategies that strengthen organizational synergy and build more inclusive cultures in support of institutional goals.

ALVIN EVANS SERVES AS A HIGHER EDUCATION PRACTICE LEADER WITH HigherEd Talent. With more than twenty years of executive-level experience in complex local education agencies and doctoral extensive institutions of higher education, he works with organizations seeking to develop strategic and cutting-edge organizational capabilities. Evans's expertise lies in core human resources administrative functions (talent management, total rewards programs, professional development, information systems, labor and employee relations, contract negotiation and administration, equal employment opportunity issues, and

Affirmative Action), policy development, organizational design and development, program evaluation, change management, organizational diversity, coaching and mentoring programs and leveraging qualitative and quantitative data to enhance organizational efficiency and effectiveness. Evans is recognized by his peers as a thought leader and an award-winning author. His publications focus on leadership, organizational development, and diversity, equity, and inclusion. In addition, Evans is a sought-after speaker at educational and diversity symposia and conferences.

Printed in the USA
CPSIA information can be obtained
at www.ICGtesting.com
CBHW061520130624
10031CB00003B/60

9 781612 498379